Predestine
For Greatness

Predestine For Greatness

Rashieda F. Timpson

Library of Congress Control Number: 2019908873
ISBN: Hardcover   978-1-7960-4422-5
                  Softcover   978-1-7960-4421-8
                  eBook   978-1-7960-4420-1

Scripture quotations marked NIV are taken from the Holy Bible, New International Version®. NIV®. Copyright © 1973, 1978, 1984 by International Bible Society. Used by permission of Zondervan. All rights reserved. [Biblica]

Unless otherwise indicated, all scripture quotations are from The Holy Bible, English Standard Version® (ESV®). Copyright ©2001 by Crossway Bibles, a division of Good News Publishers. Used by permission. All rights reserved.

Scripture quotations marked KJV are from the Holy Bible, King James Version (Authorized Version). First published in 1611. Quoted from the KJV Classic Reference Bible, Copyright © 1983 by The Zondervan Corporation.

Scripture quotations marked NLT are taken from the Holy Bible, New Living Translation, copyright © 1996, 2004, 2007. Used by permission of Tyndale House Publishers, Inc. Carol Stream, Illinois 60188. All rights reserved. Website

Print information available on the last page.

Rev. date: 07/08/2019

To order additional copies of this book, contact:
Xlibris
1-888-795-4274
www.Xlibris.com
Orders@Xlibris.com
794209

CONTENTS

I dedicate this book to God; my husband, Telly; and my beautiful children, Antwuan, Martwuan, Nakyia, and Amari. I love you all!

From a Husband's Heart

How can I describe an individual who is beyond words? Awesome! The story of your life before I met you and the story that continues before my eyes when I married you—it was just mind-blowing. I knew you were destined to do great things, and you are only scratching the surface of your potential. Your life experiences shaped your character into the woman I see daily as I rise. I am very blessed to be connected to you in this journey to greatness in God.

Love, your husband,
Telly T. Timpson

Preface

Have you ever wondered if your life was meant to be more than what it is right now? Have you ever had this unshakeable feeling that you were meant to do something great? Well, I am here to inform you those feelings are accurate; you were created with purpose on purpose! Those feelings you are experiencing is because you have greatness locked inside you. It is trying to break free, but there is something holding you back! What is it?

Ever since the foundation of the world, we have been fighting an enemy that has been trying to diminish the greatness that is inside all of us. The Bible says in John 10:10 that the enemy comes to steal, kill, and destroy, so the enemy wants to rob you of the destiny that has been already prepared for you. He wants to kill the gifts and talents that has been given to you by God and destroy any thought of you becoming successful. I have come to let you know that you are predestined for greatness! God told the prophet Jeremiah that before he was in his mother's womb, he knew him and set him apart and appointed him to be a prophet to the nations (Jer. 1:5), so God has called you and had a plan for you before you were even born!

This book is to encourage you that no matter what has happened in your past to try to discourage you from becoming successful, it will not stop you from reaching your highest dreams. The negative things that have happened in your life were a plot from the enemy to try and stop you from discovering your God-given purpose. After reading this book, you will be confident and reassured that what you have been through was all a setup for you to walk right into your destiny!

Acknowledgments

I would like to thank God the Father, God the Son, and God the Holy Spirit. Without them, there would be no book. There would be no me. I am grateful to the Father for creation, and I thank Him for creating me before I was in my mother's womb and calling me to be a prophet for this nation. I thank the Son, Jesus Christ, for dying for my sins so I can be redeemed. I thank the Holy Spirit for changing me and using me for God's glory. I thank you, Holy Spirit, for helping me write this book.

I would like to thank my wonderful husband, Telly, for loving me just for me, for not judging me by my past, and for being a demonstration of God's unconditional love to me. I would like to thank my beautiful children, Antwuan, Martwuan, Nakyia, and Amari. You are God's gifts to me, and I pray that my life, my story, will be an example as you follow your own journey, that you all will deepen your relationship with God, and that it will propel you to walk in your own destiny.

I would like to thank my mother and father, Pamela and Kevin. Without you both, I would not be here. Thank you, Mom, for always being there and supporting me. I would like to thank my grandmother, who helped raise me and who saw firsthand how God changed my life—thank you, Jean, for putting up with me through my worst times. To my sisters—Brandy, Candice, Jessica, and Jocelyn—you all knew me and knew my past and my path.

I would like to thank my spiritual father, Willie C. H. Garrett, for showing me a new way of thinking in God and pushing me to new levels. I want to thank my Aunt Faye, who invited me to church, and when I decided to stay for a while, you showed me the ropes. I would like to thank all my family and friends.

Last but not least, I want to thank those who purchased this book and who have supported the ministry over the years. I pray this book blesses you and helps you move in the next level in God for your life. Many blessings to you all!

Chapter 1

There Is Greatness Locked Inside You

You, dear children, are from God and have overcome them, because
the one who is in you is greater than the one who is in the world.
—1 John 4:4 NIV

There is greatness inside you.

Since we were born, we have been dealing with an enemy who has been trying his best efforts to cause our demise. We have been presented with situations that sometimes have been out of our control; we have faced oppositions, problems, challenges, and issues that can cause us to lose hope, dictate our actions, shape our character, and alter our destiny. When we were children, we had a set of issues that was based on what our intellectual minds could handle at that time. Our problems could have been based on trying new things and falling into pitfalls that were centered on trying to identify who we were. Our issues could've been based on our surroundings, our parents, or our family.

When we were adolescents, most of our decisions were determined by someone else because we were too young to comprehend. We learned by what we saw and what was taught to us, which sometimes was a good thing or a bad thing.

When we became teenagers, we had a little more autonomy because our parents or loved ones were not with us all the time. We started developing our own thoughts and made our own decisions based on what we obtained as a child. When you add this with what we learned from our peers, it shaped what we perceived was happening in our world. This also shaped who we thought we should be.

Then we reached adulthood, what we have learned from the cradle until now shaped our thought process. We think we have it all together, we know what we should do, and we know what direction we should take. We know, we know, and we know some more; and no one can tell us anything.

The problem with this scenario is that along the way, just as we learned good things, we also learned some not-so-good things. We have learned habits that were beneficial and habits that were not. Just like the Bible talks about good seeds that can be sewn into our lives to reap a harvest, on the flip side, the enemy has sown bad seeds in our minds, which affects our actions and corrupts our beliefs about who we think we are.

Let me explain. When you were a child, someone probably didn't like you, for whatever reason that might have been. In your mind, you might have started wondering what you might have done for them not to like you. Another scenario is that your parents might have abandoned you or maybe they did not show you any affection, so now you're struggling to find love in all the wrong places. You might not have been the most popular person in school. You were not picked to be in the cool kids' club and sit at their table at lunch, so now you are struggling to find acceptance. All these scenarios can lead to having doubts about yourself and feeling inadequate about who you are.

As a teen, you might have dealt with rejection. You might have followed after the crowd even when you knew it was wrong. You might have made bad decisions based on other people's thoughts and opinions of you. These are some of the seeds the enemy has set up in our lives to cause us to damage our character and to try to alter our destiny.

Now that we are adults, and based off our experiences and what we think we should know, we believe we have it all figured out, but we fail to realize that those negative seeds have set in and have taken root in the inner core of our soul, and it is controlling our very being. We are now puppets to the negative seeds that have sprouted up, directing our every move and dictating our future.

Because of the countless failures, disappointments, rejections, and oppressions, we have developed a sense of inadequacy; and now we can't move forward because those seeds have taken root and we are stuck! This inhibits us from walking in the purpose that God has for us.

Today is the day you become free because God has the ability to uproot those negative strongholds that are in your life, and then you will be able to tap into the greatness that's locked inside you!

The Bible declares in 1 John 4:4 that "greater is the one that is in you, than the one that is in the world." This means that God's Holy Spirit dwells inside you. The enemy wants you to believe you have no power over him, but God says He has given us power, dominion, and authority to trample over scorpions and snakes and power over all the attacks of the enemy (Luke 10:19). This means God has given us more power than we think. The enemy likes to come in and try to invoke fear in our lives. He wants us to believe we are powerless when it's the total opposite—we are powerful! We have to understand that it's not our power we're operating in. It is the power of God. When we try to work in our own power, that's when we are defeated. It's only through the power of God that we are made powerful. I always say this: you cannot go into a spiritual fight fleshly thinking. Meaning, we are not fighting a war in the natural sense, but it's the spiritual war that is going on. The Bible declares, "For our struggle is not against flesh and blood, but against the rulers, against the authorities, against the powers of this dark world and against the spiritual forces of evil in the heavenly realms" (Eph. 6:12 NIV). So when you try to fight the devil with natural means, this is when you will fail. Jesus told us that He will send a helper, which is the Holy Spirit, and that is where we draw our strength. This concept shows the whole purpose of "greater is he that is in you than he that is in the world." Greater is this Holy Spirit that is within you than the devil, his tactics, and his schemes that are in the world. The greatness is locked inside you, and you need to unlock it to reach your full potential.

We have been operating in fleshly and carnal thinking. God wants us to tap into the Holy Spirit. This is where we can have dominion, power, and authority. We thank God for Jesus because in Him we're able to overcome the flesh and tap into the Spirit of God. We can do this by putting off the old man and putting on the new man. What does this mean?

Earlier we talked about how, since the very beginning of our being, we have been taught a set of behaviors. We have formulated our own way of doing things through our own thought processes because of experiences we have obtained along the way. From childhood to adulthood, whether good, bad, or indifferent, we have learned behaviors obtained through experiences and from what we were taught. Some of those experiences were good; some of those were bad. Some things we were taught were beneficial, and some were not. Ultimately, it has shaped who we are, but some things we obtained do not line up with the will of God for our lives. God knew this was going to happen. That's why He tells us we are made anew once we are in Christ. Second Corinthians 5:17 (NIV) says, "Therefore, if anyone is in Christ, the new creation has come: The old has gone, the new is here!" This shows us that our old way of thinking must change. This lets us know that those negative seeds, those negative behaviors, and those negative concepts we have gained in our lives must fade away. We are in Christ, and He allows our minds to be ridden of evil and negative thoughts, which can corrupt our character.

Our minds have the capacity to be renewed daily, and it must line up with the mind of Christ (Phil. 2:5–11). By being a new creation in Christ, we can rejoice because it does not matter how we grew up, it does not matter what negative experiences we have faced, it does not matter what we have done in the past, it does not matter who likes us or not, and it does not matter what people think because all that matters is what God thinks about us. He loves us enough to make us in the image of Him. He loves us enough to give us power, dominion, and authority in this earth (Gen. 1:26–28). We are able to cast down every imagination that does not line up with the Word of God. God says you're more than a conqueror (Rom. 8:37), God says you're the head and not the tail (Deut. 28:13), and God says you are loved (John 3:16), and that's all that matters in the eyes of God.

There is greatness inside you, and you have the ability through God to uproot every negative seed or root that has been planted in your life because greater is He that is in you than he that is in the world!

Chapter 2

The Early Years

Then he had another dream, and he told it to his brothers.
"Listen," he said, "I had another dream, and this time the sun
and moon and eleven stars were bowing down to me.
—Gen. 37:9 NIV

"Lady Ann, oh, Lady Ann!" my mother shouted as I ran from my bedroom and dashed across the living room into my parents' master bedroom, breathing heavily, gasping for air while attempting to smile at the same time, and focusing all my attention on my parents. "Lady Ann, can you please get me a glass of water?" I was so happy to get what my mother requested. This was a little game my parents played to get me to do something quickly and efficiently. I loved serving, I loved doing things for people, and I loved to see the smile and excitement on their faces as I stopped what I was doing at that time to serve them. This started when I was about four years old; I remember it vividly because I was not even in school yet. One Christmas, my parents decided to buy my sister and me a children's Bible. I was amazed by the stories, and we started praying to God at night and trying to do well in His sight, even though my parents never taught us biblical principles or took us to church. In my early years of childhood, I always knew I was someone special. I used to have dreams and visions that I would save the world one day, like a superhero, or invent something that would change the world. I was so fascinated about the world and everything that was in it. I knew I was meant to do something great; I knew I had a purpose on this earth, and I was determined to find out what that purpose was going to be!

A. J. Enterprise, Fifty-First Street, South Side, Chicago

When I was about six years old, my grandmother used to take me to the shop she owned in the South Side of Chicago. It was called A. J. Enterprises. She sold hair products and other items for the African American community. I loved going with my grandmother to her shop. It was a long ride from Harvey, Illinois, where we stayed, to the South Side because she never took the expressway. I did not know it at the time that we had to take the long way to the shop because she did not like driving on the expressway; I found this out when I became older. All I knew was that it felt like forever to get there. I made sure I did not drink any liquids and used the bathroom before I left because I did not want to prolong the trip by asking my grandmother to stop so I could go to the bathroom.

It was a long but peaceful ride. She would put in her favorite gospel tape. It was Shirley Caesar. I would hear songs like "No Charge" and "Hold My Mule." I would hear those songs and start singing along with Shirley, imagining I was right there with her in the stories she told. I knew them by heart because I heard the songs over and over every time I got into my grandmother's car.

These songs were different than the songs I used to hear on the radio with my parents. They produced a different effect. I was happier. I felt more hopeful. I measured how long it would take to get to my grandmother's shop by how long the cassette tape played. When one side of the tape was finished and she flipped it over to the other side and it played almost halfway through, we were almost there.

When we arrived at her shop, she would unlock the metal screen that shielded the glass door by taking off the big round silver metal lock that kept the brown metal screen secured in its place. Then she would remove the metal screen from the large window, which protected people from breaking it.

I loved going to my grandmother's shop. There's something about your family owning their own shop or store. Every time someone walked in the store, I would get this feeling like, "Yes, this is my grandmother's store, and everything that's in here I can ask, and she would give it to me without paying." I did not ask for much, but it felt good that when I did ask, she would give it to me.

My grandmother's brother also owned a business. It was right on the corner from my grandmother's shop. We called him Junior—well, Uncle Junior to me. He owned a convenience store that sold liquor, quick snacks, and household items that you may have ran out of and just needed a replacement until you get to the large grocery store, like dishwashing liquid or bars of soap. This was one of the reasons I loved going to my grandmother's shop because I could walk about twenty sidewalk squares (that's what I thought as a kid) and I was at Uncle Junior's shop. He would see me coming and give me a big kiss on the cheek. I loved him. He always treated me and my sister with kindness, and he would give us whatever we wanted in the store. I would get the same thing all the time—a big dill pickle in a plastic bag out of the big jar on the store counter and a Klondike ice cream bar. My request became so redundant that when he saw me walk into the store, he automatically said, "Go ahead and get the Klondike bar and a pickle." I happily walked over to get my items, sat in the store for a little bit, and walked back to my grandmother's shop, counting the squares on the sidewalk.

My granny's shop was located on Fifty-First Street of South Side, Chicago. There were many businesses on this street. On the weekends, it was very busy. People would walk outside, go in and out of shops, and enjoy their day. These businesses were owned by African American people, and they were doing well for themselves.

One time I was looking out the window of my grandmother's shop on the busy street, and I saw a pink Cadillac driving slowly down Fifty-First Street with hundreds of people following along. I ran outside to see who it was in the pink Cadillac, and to my surprise, it was Mr. T. I started waving my hand, shouting "Mr. T! Mr. T!" hoping he would see me in the sea of people. It was awesome to see a celebrity who was from my hometown riding down the street, waving to the people. He looked just like he did on *The A-Team*—gold chains around his neck, an Afro-Mohawk, and sleeveless shirt. It felt great to see someone who looked like me who was rich and famous—well, at least I thought he was rich. I was thinking to myself, *One day, I will be an important person too, but I will use what I have to change the world.* I was a little girl with enormous dreams.

I was an outgoing little girl. I was not shy. I was very outspoken and loved to help. One day I asked my grandmother if I could help sell her products. My grandmother put a little table in front of the shop and put some products and little knickknacks like children toys and so forth so I could attempt to sell. I would see people walking down the street and invite them to my table—I didn't take no for an answer. I would tell them why they needed the products I was selling and they should buy it. Most people did. Now that I think about it, it was not so much what I was selling but who was selling it. I was a cute little six-year-old girl who was outgoing and outspoken, and I was not going to let them leave without buying at least one of the items on the table. I realized later that this was a gift. I was a people person. I loved people, and I loved communicating with people. I loved having a sense of purpose. I did not want to just sit around and do nothing while other people were working. My grandmother saw that I was good at this, so every time I came to the shop, she would put a table out for me and put products on the table; and I would do it all over again, except if it was cold outside or raining. I would say to the people, "Come over and see what you must buy." I was now my own little businessperson in my own kid kind of way.

The South Side of Chicago was not always the most prime place to be. It was a little rough around the edges. One day I was in Kentucky Fried Chicken (now called KFC) and a guy walked in. He took something out of his long, dark-tan trench coat, walked up to the cashier, and demanded money. They put it in a paper bag, and then the man ran out. I was about seven years old. I sat there not scared but kind of confused at what had happened because it was so fast. The employees did not let us leave for about twenty minutes, until the police came. I had already placed my order; I was just waiting for the food. So I walked up to the register and said, "Am I able to still get my food?"

This same thing happened another time at the same Kentucky Fried Chicken about four months later. After that, my grandmother stopped me from walking to get food for lunch. My grandmother would not get anymore chicken from KFC; she would go to Harold's Chicken instead. I thought they were better anyway.

How Did I End Up There?

I was a kid that loved the outdoors. I made my choices, and if I was not punished for not doing what I was supposed to do, I was able to go outside and play. Back then, we could go outside and leave our block as long as we came back home to check in with our parents, and we definitely had to be in the house when the streetlights came on. The streetlights were our cue that we better get our butts in the house or we would be in some trouble. Sometimes, when the streetlights came on, we would play in front of the house or I would go to my friend's house around the corner and play in front of her house because my parents knew their parents well.

One day, I cannot even recall how I ended up there, but one Sunday morning, I must have woken up early and started riding my bike down a couple of blocks. There was this big church about two blocks from where I lived, and it sat on a corner. It was a brown brick-like establishment with stained glass windows. I do not recall if I knocked on the door or if someone asked if I wanted to come in, but I winded up in the church on a Sunday morning before service. I can remember it was about 9:30 a.m., and someone led me up the stairs to a well-lit room with rows of chairs lined perfectly. Each chair had a book. They instructed me to open the book and turn to a page. I had never done this before, but I liked it. They sang songs about God and Jesus. I thought, *This is the same feeling that I get when I go to my grandmother's shop listening to*

Shirley Caesar. The feeling made me happy. After the singing session was over, they asked me if I wanted to go downstairs to have doughnuts and juice. I gladly shook my head up and down, and next thing I knew, I was eating a glazed doughnut and drinking orange juice from a Styrofoam cup. After eating my sweet treat and drinking my juice, it was time for church service. I never experienced this before. All I remember was that I was in the back, sitting on the brown pew, and next thing I knew, I was curled in a ball on the pew and fast asleep. I woke up, and it was just ending, so I exited the building, hopped on my bike, and headed home. I woke my mom up and told her where I had been. She just said "Oh, that's nice" and went back to sleep. I thought, *I will be back next Sunday.*

This was a routine for me every Sunday—singing, eating doughnuts, drinking juice, and then church service; but this time, instead of going to sleep right before church service started, I waited for them to pass the church collection plate around. It was a shiny gold plate that was deep in the center. It had a dark-red velvet patch in the center. I made sure I looked around the house for any change I could find and put it in the plate. I did not focus on the amount. The change consisted of mostly pennies, but it did not matter. I was just happy when the gold plate with the dark-red velvet center came to me; I had something to put in there. After that, I fell asleep.

Once a month, the church would have a full dinner. I looked forward to these days. I tried to get my sister to come with me on some Sundays, but she never wanted to get up on time. I didn't care if she did not go; I was going. I was the type of kid who was spontaneous. If I set my mind to do something, I would do it. I did not care if others did not want to do it; if I wanted to do it, it was going to be done.

When I think about this time in my life, I believe God was sending me there for a purpose. The seed was planted within me by singing the songs in the morning before doughnuts and juice and being in the midst of the Word when it was preached, even if I fell asleep. I sowed my own destiny by putting the pennies that I so eagerly searched for around the house to put in the gold collection plate with the dark-red velvet patch in the middle. It did not matter how much I was giving; what mattered was I was giving with a cheerful heart.

At this stage in my life, I looked at the world through rose-colored glasses; meaning, I thought everything was like a fairy tale. I was a little girl who was happy and found ways to be happy. I was in control of my happiness, and I loved people. I dreamed big. I thought, *I know I will be used to change the world, I know I will.*

Then things started to change. Something happened to that loving little girl who trusted everybody, who loved people, and who loved serving. Something happened that this little girl was ashamed to talk about. This was just the beginning of the end of that sweet little girl, not all at once, but a slow fade of losing sight and insight of who she was and the purpose that was attached to her. A seed of negativity was planted and started to take root in the very depths of her soul.

As I reflect on the earlier years of my life, Genesis 37 comes to mind. The story of Joseph is a well-known story I often refer to when I look back at my childhood. Joseph had two dreams showing that he would be in a position of authority. God had shown him that he would be in a situation where he would be ruler of his brothers and even his mother and father. When he told his dreams to his brothers, it made them hate him even more because he was favored by their father. Joseph did not know the full purpose in his life, but based on the dreams he had, he knew he was meant to be someone great.

God speaks to all of us in different ways, just like I had a feeling I was meant to do something great but did not know at the time the fullness of what that greatness was. God knows what we are purposed to do, but it might take a while for us to realize what that purpose is. When you know you are supposed to do something great with your life, it opens the door for the enemy to use anyone to stop you from reaching your destiny. Just like Joseph's brothers hated him for being favored by their father and telling his dreams, we have an enemy who hates the fact that God has called us from the spiritual realm to be manifested on earth to fulfill the purpose we were called to do. It is the same with the first man and woman, Adam and Eve. As soon as the Lord told them their purpose—which was to be fruitful and multiply and to replenish the earth, subdue it, and have dominion over it—the enemy came shortly after to rob them of their destiny (Gen. 1:28).

We have to understand that when we are called to do something great, evil forces will try to stop us from reaching our goal, living out our dreams, and walking in our purpose; but Let us be reminded of the scripture in 1 John 4:4 (NIV): "You, dear children, are from God and have overcome them, because the one who is in you is greater than the one who is in the world." Keep on dreaming because our dreams will manifest if we do not lose hope.

Chapter 3

A Dark Moment, Then a Glimpse of Light

The weapons we fight with are not the weapons of the world. On the contrary, they have divine power to demolish strongholds.
—2 Cor. 10:4 (NIV)

When I was about seven or eight years old (not sure on the age because for years I tried to block it from my memory), I was on summer vacation, and my sister and I went to my great-grandmother's house for the summer. I loved going there. This was something we did almost every summer, but this time, my parents sent us to Ohio to spend the summer without them. At my great-grandmother's house, there was always someone home—cousins, uncles, or friends of the family. Her house was an open door, and she treated everyone like family. That was just the type of person she was.

One night, a friend of the family was over one of my family member's house. He came in to where I was sleeping and asked me to come downstairs in another part of the house. I was young, and everyone was always friendly, so I did not think anything bad was going to happen. Then it happened. This person started touching and fondling me inappropriately. I was confused and scared, and I did not know what to do. I just went along with it. After it was over, the person told me not to tell anyone, that it was "our little secret." This went on four to five times during my summer vacation there. Fear gripped my mind. I wanted to tell someone, but what if no one believed me? I felt embarrassed, ashamed, dirty, and sad.

We went back home after the summer vacation was over, and I did not tell a soul, not even my sister, whom I told everything to. This was something I had to put deep down in my mind, forget, get over, and act like it did not happen. In my mind, it never did, but the seed had been planted. Little did I know, this was just the beginning of the deterioration of knowing who I thought I was to become. When I returned to Illinois, I had placed the memory of me being sexually fondled so far back in my mind it was like it never happened at all, and I went on with my life.

Mrs. Thornton, the Seed-Bearer

One day, a group of my friends and I were walking down the street, playing around as usual, being adventurous, and trying to find something to do. We often made up our own games and stayed out of the house because most of our parents had already warned us if we kept running in and out the house, we would have to stay in. I never understood the concept of that—did it really bother them that we came in and out of the house? We often just stayed outside the whole day because we did not want to be stuck in the house with our boring parents. If we needed a drink of water, we would get the water hose at the side of the house, and that was just as good as the faucet. The water was cold with a hint of a metallic taste, and it felt good while it was running down our dry throats. We did what we could not to go in the house and take the risk that we would be in the way.

My friends and I, including my oldest sister, were walking down the street when this van pulled up at the side of us. A well-dressed older lady with glasses hopped out of the car and said, "Hi, my name is Mrs. Thornton, do you all want to be in a children's choir?" We all looked at each other and said sure. I didn't even know what a children's choir was; I knew it had to do with children being in church. As I pondered on what this could be all about, my mind went back to when I went to the church down the street. I remembered that, after I ate my doughnut and drank my orange juice, I would go upstairs to the big room with the colorful stained glass windows and long brown benches. Just before I fell asleep, I would see people on what looked like a stage wearing the same clothes, which looked like a plain dress, and they were singing songs like the ones by Shirley Caesar, which I listened to in my grandmother's car on the way to her shop in South Side.

I thought, *Maybe this is what we would be doing in this children's choir.* This made me want to go even more, and I was always spontaneous, and my friend were too, so we were up for the challenge. In addition to we were always looking for things to do, so this was definitely something to do. She then gave us a permission slip with her contact information and told us to give it to our parents and have them sign and give her a call.

The next week, Mrs. Thornton pulled up in front of our house and picked us up to take us to our first choir practice. When we arrived at the church, there were other kids already there. She began explaining to us that we would be singing songs on certain Sundays during church service. We started to learn songs like "This Little Light of Mine," "How Majestic Is Your Name," "Walking Up the King's Highway," and "Jesus Loves Me." Mrs. Thornton would pick us up faithfully every week and take us to practice. This one girl who was not a part of my group of friends would always get the lead part. Her name, let's just call her Angel. I would wonder why she would always get the lead. Was it because her name was a name that identified with church? Well, she did have a nice voice, but I thought that I would like to get a lead part one day. But the more I thought about it, the more I started to become fearful of singing a lead part in front of a large congregation. Where did this fear come from? I used to be so outspoken. Where was the little girl who had her own table in front of her grandmother's store on the South Side of Chicago, who directed people, total strangers, over to her table to buy things she felt they needed? This was a change.

I never spoke up and asked Mrs. Thornton if I could have a solo part. I just stayed in the background. Even though I was in the background, I felt joy when I sang the songs. I had the same feeling I used to have when I was singing gospel songs in my grandmother's car on the way to the shop—feelings of joy and happiness. I was hopeful. It brought me peace, and I was grateful that, one day, a little old lady by the name of Mrs. Thornton stopped by a group of kids and asked if they would be a part of a children's choir. She did not know us; she did not know our parents. She did not know we would even accept the invitation. I believe God used her on that day to sow a seed in my life that would one day sprout up.

Seeds from the Enemy

The sexual assault that happened when I was a child planted seeds of fear and shame. This was the start of what I call a deep-rooted stronghold. A stronghold is something that has been planted deep down in your mind that can help shape your character and your way of thinking. Many of us have, in some form or fashion, encountered a stronghold in our lives. If you just take a look into my situation when I was a kid, that one encounter caused me to experience several negative emotions and perceptions, which stayed with me well into my adult years. Because of those negative emotions and perceptions, it shaped how I viewed and treated relationships. The enemy tactic is the same— try and plant negative seeds at a young age to try and derail the person from knowing who they are in God and to stop them from walking in power and authority.

Strongholds as a child can come in many forms such as shame, doubt, fear, embarrassment, anger, abandonment, guilt, and countless other negative emotions. As a child, it is hard to channel negative emotions into positive emotions because the human brain in not yet fully developed. A child processes their thinking differently than an adult. Children lack that abstract thinking, which causes one to think more in-depth. They are more engaged in concrete thinking, which focuses on the here and now, which causes them to believe what they are feeling at that moment is actual, factual, and the way it is supposed to be. That's why it is important to tell your child to come and talk with you if they are having issues, if something happened to them that made them feel scared or ashamed so you can address the issues right away. Because of my experiences in life, I always tell my kids to be open and honest about feelings they may have that are negative so I can address the issue and stop the stronghold from growing.

A stronghold is not something that you can deal with in the natural realm of things; this is a spiritual war that has to be dealt with the Word of God and with prayer. First, you have to identify where the stronghold came from and what it is and have faith through prayer and speaking the Word that you will bring that stronghold down. If you are fearful of something, by faith you can speak the Word that says, "For the Spirit God gave us does not make us timid, but gives us power, love and self-discipline.

"(2 Tim. 1:7 NIV).

The enemy wants situations and circumstances to happen in your life to stop you from your purpose. Those strongholds are meant to stay in your mind to hold you back back from future progress. See, if Satan can get you when you are kid, he has a running start to stop your purpose. What do I mean "a running start"? This means he can get to you before you even acknowledge or even know who you are in God.

When we are young, we don't even have a clue of what God has for us in His totality in our lives. We're still trying to find our identity. And the devil can come and stop us from knowing who we are in God— that's when he has a running start to try to snatch the very purpose that was ordained for our lives.

You have the ability to overcome those negative events in your life, and you have the ability to move forward in your purpose and the destiny that was designed for your life. Just imagine this: Individuals who are entrepreneurs or innovators often have a plan for what they want to see to come to pass. They know what they want to do and what they want to accomplish. Even though they have this plan or blueprint, they often run into bumps on the road. Even though they have the plan laid out in front of them, they often run into problems or issues along the way. This does not stop them from reaching their goals and dreams. This does not stop them from accomplishing what was written on the blueprint. This causes them to fight harder because they know there is something greater that's going to come out of this.

Let's look at the life of Thomas Edison. He made one thousand unsuccessful attempts at inventing the light bulb. When a reporter asked, "How did it feel to fail one thousand times?" Edison replied, "I didn't fail one thousand times. The light bulb was an invention with one thousand steps." On the 1,001st time, he got it correct, and we are all enjoying the fruits of his tenacity today! This is no different between you and me.

God has a blueprint for our lives. He has a purpose and destiny for our lives. Even if the plan is laid out in front of us, there will be hiccups along the way and there will be problems that occur, but this should not stop us from reaching our goals and from reaching our dreams. If we are already predestined for greatness, it means it was already written; we just have to play it out.

The enemy wants to confuse us and to derail us from what God has already written for our lives. We were already meant to win, so we must tap into the Holy Spirit through the power of God to continue to move forward with what God has for us, regardless of what has happened in our youth, our teenage years, and our adulthood. We have the ability to overcome challenges and circumstances if we do not allow those negative things that happened to us to hold us back. So for those negative strongholds that has been planted in our minds, we pray against them in the name of Jesus. They are no longer planted in our minds. We call on the power and authority of Jesus Christ to snatch them out of our lives; we no longer will fight this battle by natural means, but we call on the Holy Spirit to eliminate those negative seeds that have taken root in our lives.

Seeds Planted by God

Even though negative seeds were planted by the enemy when I was a child. God came along and planted seeds to help me overcome the effects of what the enemy had tried to do. The devil wants us to be fearful and be ashamed of things that has happened our lives, whether it was out of our control or not. Now that I am in Christ, I know for a fact that God sent Mrs. Thornton to get me back to what drew me to Him in the first place. By singing those songs in the children's choir, it gave me hope, joy, and peace. I felt a sense of God's love for me. The Bible says that the Lord will never leave us or forsake us (Heb. 13:5). This means that when we feel like we are all alone, God is always there. He was reminding me that He loves me, and He will always give me hope in the midst of trouble.

God will send people to sow good seeds in your life, which will bear fruit at a later time. God always backs up what He says with scripture. Let's take a look at 1 Corinthians 3:6 (NIV) and see what it says about God sending people to plant and water seeds in our lives: "I planted the seed, Apollos watered it, but God has been making it grow." The Apostle Paul is telling us that God will use whom He will to plant seeds in our lives, but it is the Father Himself that will make those seeds grow. God has been planting seeds from the very beginning.

We tend to always look at the bad things that has happened in our lives. For example, we tend to focus on all the negative things and think about them over and over. This causes us to continue to relive that negative moment and causes the negative seed to continue to grow in our lives. The Bible says that whatever you think in your heart so is he (Prov. 23:7). So if we keep dwelling on things that have hurt us in the past, those feelings of fear, resentment, bitterness, anger, sadness, and depression will continue to dwell in our hearts; and it will control our actions. Let's take a look at what the Bible says you should do when it comes to your thinking:

> Finally, brothers and sisters, whatever is true, whatever is noble, whatever is right, whatever is pure, whatever is lovely, whatever is admirable—if anything is excellent or praiseworthy—think about such things. Whatever you have learned or received or heard from me or seen in me—put it into practice. And the God of peace will be with you. (Phil. 4:8–9 NIV)

Apostle Paul is telling us that we must think on good things. When we think of good things, we will obtain the peace of God. I remember one time, I continued to think about a situation in my life, and it had me bound. I started to worry, and I started to become fearful. I could not sleep at night. Then I went to God in prayer and said, "Lord, why does this situation continue to plague me?" He said so clearly, "Daughter, what have you been thinking about?" Then He reminded me of Philippians 4:8–9. I knew this scripture by heart because after every church service that I was asked to close out, I spoke this very scripture. So right then I knew what the problem was—I was thinking on the wrong things. God is saying to think on the right things and you will have peace. Just like God said in Isaiah 26:3 (NIV), "You will keep in perfect peace those whose minds are steadfast, because they trust in you."

Those Negative Seeds Grow with the Positive

When you think about a harvest, crops, or something you plant in the ground, you would expect that whatever you have planted would spring forth in its due season. If you plant tomatoes, you expect tomatoes. If you plant corn, you expect corn; but oftentimes, things grow with whatever you planted, and it is an unwanted plant such as weeds. Weeds reduce farm and forest productivity. They invade crops, smother pastures, and in some cases, harm livestock. They aggressively compete for water, nutrients, and sunlight, resulting in reduced crop yield and poor crop quality. This is the same when you have good seeds that were planted from God and bad seeds that were planted by the enemy. The seeds of hurt, pain, rejection, fear, bitterness, and anger will try and smother the good seeds such as love, joy, and peace that were planted in the very beginning our existence. That is why it is so important to get rid of those negative things that have taken root in us to prevent the corruption of the good seeds that will spring up in our lives.

The Bible talks about the fruit of the Spirit. It's found in Galatians 5:22–23 (NIV), and it states, "But the fruit of the Spirit is love, joy, peace, forbearance, kindness, goodness, faithfulness, gentleness and self-control." This is the fruit that should be manifested in our lives. That is why it is important to ask God to remove those weeds that came from the enemy's seeds, which will try and hinder the fruit of the Spirit from growing in our lives.

Chapter 4

Seeds of Rejection

But you are a chosen people, a royal priesthood, a holy nation,
God's special possession, that you may declare the praises of him
who called you out of darkness into his wonderful light.

—1 Pet. 2:9 NIV

I was so eager to start school because my sister, who was eighteen months older than me, always bragged about how fun school was. When you are in grade school, you're supposed to have peers that you connect with. This was supposed to be a fun and exciting time, finding your place in your own little world without any worries or cares. This lasted for me up until the fifth grade. The problem started when I did not have the things the other kids had. We were not poor, but my parents felt it was not necessary to have expensive things. I did not wear the latest shoes or clothes, so I was not among the popular group. I wanted to be cool, noticed, and popular like the other kids; so I reverted to what I knew, trying to do things to make people happy like I did with my parents in the little game we played when they called me Lady Ann. I did things for attention. I did things for my so-called friends for them to be happy for a moment, and then once the happiness wore off, they wouldn't even notice me.

I can remember an incident when my sister's best friend did my hair. Wearing hair extensions, or hairweave, was not popular back then because it was so new. My sister's friend did my hair into two curly ponytails, one on the side of my hair and one on the back of my head. I looked in the mirror and thought, *I look so pretty, but what are people going to say when I go to school?* I was very nervous when I went to school, even somewhat fearful. Would they say things like "Give that horse his hair back"? Where was the little girl in my earlier years who was so bold, so confident? Where was she? Clearly, she was not with me these days. I went to school the next day with a lump in my throat. My stomach turned, and I felt nauseated as I approached my classroom. I took a deep breath and entered the crowded room and took my seat in the third row. All eyes were on me, and it seemed at the time that every eye on me was burning through my soul. Then I heard some classmates say, "Wow, your hair is cute!" I sighed in relief as the teacher started to speak on the lesson for the day.

About midway through the day, two of the so-called popular girls who were sitting behind me said, "Rashieda, who did your hair? What is it made of?" The girl that said it, along with her friend, started laughing. I told her my sister's friend did my hair, and that's what it's made of. Then she took out her scissors and cut a piece of my ponytail in the back, and she showed me. People started to laugh. I was so embarrassed, and I started to cry. I went home and took off the hair extensions from my head. My sister and her best friend were already at home, and they asked me what happened. I told my older sister, who was in junior high at the time, what happened, and she was furious. My sister and her friend were considered popular at their junior high school, and we lived in such a family community. The older siblings of the two popular girls who went to my school went to my oldest sister's school as well. My sister and her best friend were so mad about what they did to my hair. They both decided they were going up to my school the next day to confront the girls who were bullying me.

I do not believe I went to school the next day because I was so embarrassed. My sister's school dismissed classes about one hour earlier than my school, so they came home and said, "Come on, you will point out these girls who cut your hair." My school was literally two blocks from our house. I lived so close that when I got to the crossing guard for my school I saw my house. I walked slowly behind my sister and her friend, a little nervous, but a part of me was eager to see what they were going to do. When we got about halfway in the field surrounding my school, I saw the girls walking in our direction. I pointed forward and said, "There they are." My sister and her friend quickly surrounded them. I don't remember all what they said, but I know they said this, "If she tells us that you did something else to her again, you have to answer to us!" The two girls who bullied me looked so scared; I think one of them started to cry. I kind of felt sorry for them, but that was me, not caring that they just humiliated me and made me cry; instead, I was looking out for their feelings. To be completely honest, a small part of me was slightly happy. It was a chance for them to get a taste of what I went through. After that day, I never had a problem with them again.

I did not have any more issues at my school, but that did not stop issues from hitting the home front. Soon as things seemed calm, the unthinkable happened in my life. My parents separated. I was devastated. I thought, *What does this mean? What is going to happen next?*

It seemed like my world was falling apart. I felt so alone in this. I just did not understand the plan for my life. I already felt rejected by my peers, and now I have to deal with this from my own parents. I just kept hoping that this was all a bad dream and that I would soon wake up and things would be better, but this was no dream; this was reality, and I had to deal with it—I had no choice. I did not understand at the time that what was happening was still a part of God's plan even though the devil meant it for evil. I was angry and bitter; I was feeling the effects of being rejected. I thought, *Lord, is this the plan you have for me? If so, I do not understand your purpose in all this. Why do things keep happening to me!*

Rejection for Your Perfection

First, we have to understand that rejection is a part of this process. When you're a child, you can't understand that rejection can be for your benefit. You do not comprehend that rejection has always been part of the process since the very beginning. In the Bible, Jesus says that the world is going to hate you because it first hated him. John 15:18–25 makes it clear that if you belong to the world, the world will love you as its own, but because Jesus Himself has chosen us out of the world, the world will hate you. The enemy will use anyone to discourage you, talk about you, and try to get you out of your character because of the love you have for Christ. It does not matter what you may have done or if you have done anything at all. Jesus said in the book of John chapter 15 that they hated Him without reason. When I was in the world, I used to wonder why some people disliked me and lied to me for no reason, but over time, I realized it was not them but the spirit that was operating in them, and the spirit that was operating in them was not from God. The enemy used those people to persecute and to discourage me because he knew my destiny; he knew what I was going to become. If he could get me to have low self-esteem, it would have hindered my God-given authority to be in an elevated place in God. Elevated in what? Elevated in my thinking, my actions, and my abilities and being confident in who I am. I would have remained in a defective place instead of being in an elevated place of victory.

The seeds of rejection blocks areas of love and replaces it with bitterness and anger. Being rejected by your peers when you are trying to be accepted can cause you to do things out of your character and accept relationships that are not good for you. The separation of my parents added fuel to the fire. Their love was the connection of our family, and when that was broken, it left room for the enemy to bring fear, uncertainty, unforgiveness, and bitterness in my life. Families are supposed to stay together. Families are supposed to support one another, and when that was broken, it had provided a distorted concept of what family was all about.

It was not until I experienced God's unconditional love that I saw things in a different light. I did not understand what unconditional love was at first. I thought, *Wasn't all love conditional? If you love me, I love you. If I disliked you, you disliked me.* That was the concept I had of the world until I figured out what God's unchanging love was. His unconditional love means it does not matter what I do, did, or have done, He still loves me. I did not have to change to gain His love. I needed His love so I can portray this type of love to others. I found out that if no one else would ever love me in this world, God will.

God's Love Heals Rejection

Having God's love is having love unconditionally, without hypocrisy. We will never be who God wants us to be if we don't have love. Romans 12:9–21 talks about love. This says love must be true, love must be sincere, and love must be a selfless act. Love must trump evil. Even in the face of someone doing you wrong, even in the face of someone talking about you, and even in the event of people not treating you well, you still have to operate in God's love, which is one of the fruits of the Spirit. Galatians 5:22–23 (NIV) says, "But the fruit of the Spirit is love, joy, peace, forbearance, kindness, goodness, faithfulness, gentleness and self-control. Against such things there is no law." The work of the flesh is any act that is produced by human effort. In reference to love, if we love with human effort, it is an emotional act that we can easily turned on and off based on how we feel at the moment. Having God's love, which is one of the fruits of the Spirit, requires this to be a spiritual act, not an emotional feeling. This requires being in constant communication with the Lord. We cannot gain this type of love on our own; we have to let God's love work in us to provide this fruit.

How Do We Obtain God's Love?

How do we obtain God's love? The answer is, first, we have to love God. Matthew 22:37 (NIV) states, "Love the Lord your God with all your heart and with all your soul and with all your mind. This is the first and greatest commandment." Also, in Mark 12:30, it talks about loving God with all your strength. So we have to love the Lord with our total being, which means with our heart (emotional), soul (spiritual), mind (intellectual), and strength (physical). This is our total being. We must love God with everything we have, and He will pour His love upon us.

Another way that we love God is to wholeheartedly and unconditionally have the mind-set to want to please God. Just picture this: If we love a person, we automatically would want to spend time with them, do things for them, and not expect anything in return. We would want to do things to make the person happy. This is how we should be loving toward God, not just when we feel like it or just to receive something from Him. We should do things to please Him, which is following His commandments.

Obedience Is Another Way We Love God

In John 14:21 (NIV), Jesus says, "Whoever has my commands and keeps them is the one who loves me. The one who loves me will be loved by my Father, and I too will love them and show myself to them." So by obeying God's commandments, it shows we love Him because we do not want to disobey Him. First John 2:4–5 also states, "Whoever says, 'I know him,' but does not do what He commands is a liar, and the truth is not in that person. But if anyone obeys his word, love for God is truly made complete in them. This is how we know we are in him." Deuteronomy 11:13–15 also states that if we obey the Lord, we will also receive favor from Him. All that we need to know is in the Bible.

I once heard this saying: the meaning of each letter of the word *Bible* is (B) basic (I) instructions (B) before (L) leaving (E) earth. This is why Jesus talked about the two greatest commandments—we touched on one, which is God's love. The second one is just like He says in Matthew 22:39–40 (NIV): You shall love your neighbor as you love yourself on these two commandments hang all the law and the profits. So how do we love our neighbors as we love ourselves? First, we have to identify who the neighbor is. A neighbor could be anybody—you don't get to choose who we live next to. It could be an enemy, it could be the prostitute, it could be the drug dealer, it could be the one who talked about you in school, or it could be the one who picked on you at school. A neighbor could be anybody. A neighbor is no one in particular, so we have to do what the old saying says: do unto others what you will have them do unto you, but with a biblical aspect. We shouldn't harm ourselves, so we should treat others how we want to be treated even in the face of adversity.

Forgiveness Is an Act of Love

Forgiveness is another key to walk in the real love of God. There are some people who have hurt me in the past, but if I had allowed those seeds of hurt to grow in my life, I would not have been able to receive the love of God. We all make mistakes. We are not perfect, but through it all, God still loves us. Matthew 6:14 (NIV) says, "For if you forgive other people when they sin against you, your heavenly Father will also forgive you

." So if God can forgive us for our shortcomings, our issues, our mistakes, and our failures, who are we not to forgive someone else? When we forgive, it is not for that person; it is for ourselves because if we harbor unforgiveness in our lives, it will allow bitterness, anger, and resentment to overtake us and occupy the space where love is supposed to abide. God forgives our sins daily, so who are we not to forgive? If we keep those feelings of unforgiveness in our hearts, it will hold us back from loving others as well as fully loving God.

First John 4:20–21 (NIV) says, "Whoever claims to love God yet hates a brother or sister is a liar. For whoever does not love their brother and sister, whom they have seen, cannot love God, whom they have not seen. And he has given us this command: Anyone who loves God must also love their brother and sister." This scripture right here is telling us how we can love God. We have not physically seen Him yet love Him, but we hate the ones we see daily.

God is saying that those who walk in true love, love unconditionally the ones they see daily. This also means that we have to love our enemy as well. Matthew 5:43–48 (NIV) says, "You have heard that it was said, 'Love your neighbor and hate your enemy.' But I tell you, love your enemies and pray for those who persecute you, that you may be children of your Father in heaven. He causes his sun to rise on the evil and the good and sends rain on the righteous and the unrighteous. If you love those who love you, what reward will you get? Are not even the tax collectors doing that? And if you greet only your own people, what are you doing more than others? Do not even pagans do that? Be perfect, therefore, as your heavenly Father is perfect." The bottom line is that we have to be set apart. The world loves those who loves them back, but this is not the love we're seeking. If Jesus Himself, who was battered, abused, persecuted, and denied while dying on the cross, can say, "Forgive and demonstrate love unconditionally," then who are we not to return that same love?

Dealing with the seeds of rejection is an impossible task without God. These seeds come with bitterness, hatred, resentment, fear, oppression, loneliness, and anger. Situations that have happened in our lives can cause these negative seeds to be planted and grow into negative effects. In order to be healed from rejection, obtain God's love—His unconditional love. We know that forgiveness and obedience are connected to God's love. Love is one of the fruits of the Spirit, which is being in constant communication with God.

This love that I'm talking about has nothing to do with your emotional feelings but has to do with actions and tapping into the spiritual realm. The first step is forgiving those who have done you wrong and who have disappointed you. If we just think on the fact that God forgives us as we sin daily, who are we not to forgive? We have to love God with our total being through our actions, minds, thoughts, and strengths. We must be obedient to His commandments. We must love our neighbors as we love ourselves, even if that neighbor is our enemy. This does not mean being taken advantage of by those who seek to cause us harm or placing ourselves in situations that can harm us, but we must know our boundaries; and we will not allow bitterness, hatred, and resentment to fester in our lives. Sometimes we may need to love from a distance, but this takes direction from God. Most importantly, we need to learn how to love ourselves. If we don't love ourselves or forgive ourselves, how can we accurately love and forgive others?

Jesus was rejected by those who thought they had a higher position than Him. The Word says, "The stone the builders rejected has become the cornerstone; the Lord has done this, and it is marvelous in our eyes" (Matt. 21:42 NIV). The bottom-line rejection is casted out by God's love. God is love, and if we are made in the image of Him, we are love too. We must stay in communication with God through worship, prayer, and meditation on God's Word to help us gain this fruit of the Spirit. We are not perfect, and we will never be, but we must be assured that if we stay in Christ, He will continue to perfect us, which is a continuous process if we stay in connection with Him (Phil. 1:6).

Chapter 5

The Move

"For I know the plans I have for you," declares the LORD, "plans to prosper you and not to harm you, plans to give you hope and a future."
—Jer. 29:11 NIV

My parents both dealt with their own set of issues when I was a kid. No one outside the family really knew about it because they were functional, had careers, owned a house, and living the so-called American dream. When my parents decided to part ways, things seemed to get worse. I switched schools and still struggled with being accepted and still carried a people-pleaser mentality to gain friends. I moved to University Park with my mother, my two sisters, and my mother's friend, whom we've all known for years and was a big help to our family, I found out later on. I was glad to start a new school because I had such a bad experience in grade school. This time, my oldest sister was having a hard time adjusting and making new friends at the new junior high school. She was now in the eighth grade, and I was in the sixth grade. I was glad that at this school, we had to wear school uniforms because my mother never bought any brand-name clothes. She did not feel the need for it, but I did not have to worry because I was wearing uniforms anyway.

I had two friends that I had met in school, and they were also friends with each other, so we all became like the best of friends. One day, my friends got into an argument with each other. Over what? I'm not sure. I have no clue, but it was significant enough for them to go weeks without speaking—you know sixth grade–girl stuff. I would still try and maintain being both of their friends without trying to talk about one to the other, as they often talked about each other to me. One day, they decided to be friends again, and they both were saying things to each other that they had told me, but they said I had said the hurtful things. One day, they confronted me at school and said, "We decided we are not going to be your friend anymore." I tried to tell both of them that this was not true or, at least, some of it was not true to protect their innocence, but they did not listen, and they stopped being my friend that day. No more spending the night over their houses or mine. No more talking on the phone. No more playing at school. They completely ignored me. This went on for about a month. Feelings of rejection, sadness, and bitterness set in. The feelings that I knew so well came back and invaded my life. Then I started to get mad! I thought, *You know what? I don't care that they are not my friends.* I moved on, and as soon as I moved on, they both came to me saying that they decided to be my friend again. I said okay, but in all actuality, I was not interested. The friendship would never be the same. I had moved on in my mind.

Because things were dysfunctional in my home, we had the option to move to Ohio with my grandmother. At first, I was skeptical. Chicago was all I knew, but on the other hand, I thought, *What do I have to lose?* I had little to no friends, my mother and father were separated and had their own set of issues they needed to deal with, and I just wanted a change. If it took moving to Ohio, then I will do it! My sister and I agreed that we wanted to move to Ohio. We had cousins there, and we used to spend time with them every summer, so we knew some places we could visit and have fun. I thought, *We can have fun with our cousins like we did when we used to come for the summer.* But to our surprise, it did not happen the way we thought it would. Our cousins had their own lives, their own friends, and their own routines. We did not stay in the same school district as them. Here we go again, back to being rejected and alone, so I just buried myself in my video games and stayed to myself.

The Elite Teens

One day, my sister and my cousin came home with a flyer in their hands. They were bubbling with excitement as the started to talk about the flyer. The flyer stated that they were looking for teenagers to work for them and get paid daily. The organization was called the Elite Teens. They called the number on the flyer to find out more information. I can't remember if it was my cousin or my sister who called the number on the flyer to get additional information, but all I know was that they were both disappointed to find out the details of the job. The job consisted of selling candy and other items door-to-door. My cousin and my sister were not interested; they did not want any part of selling anything, especially going house to house, knocking on doors. They left the paper on the table and walked out the room. I looked at the paper and stared at it for about two minutes. They will let you work if you were at least twelve years old or eleven about to turn twelve. I thought, *This is right up my alley.* I was good at selling things. My mind went back to when I had my own table in front of my grandmother's shop on Fifty-First Street on the South Side of Chicago. My mind went to the numerous times I sold things at my school fundraisers. I was really good at it. This was a chance to make some money and buy my own clothes, shoes, etc. The way I saw it, this was my only opportunity given that I was only eleven going on twelve because in order to get a real job, I had to be fifteen with a work permit.

I called the number on the flyer and spoke with a representative for the organization. Next thing I knew, a lady, who was middle aged and had a plump built, and her husband, who was tall and slender in nature, came over to my grandmother's house and explained the program. This program was to keep teens out of trouble by giving them jobs. You went door-to-door selling candy, candles, holiday items, etc. They were in a big tote that you would carry door-to-door. Each item was four dollars, and for each item sold, you get a dollar. It does not sound like much now, but to an eleven-year-old who did not have any money, it was a lot. Before I could start working, I had to memorize the speech that we would be saying over and over as we go from house to house. It did not take me long to memorize this because I was eager to start working. I cannot remember the speech now, but I know it went on the lines of this: "Hi, my name is Rashieda, and I am a part of the Elite Teens. This is a youth program to keep kids off the streets." Then it ended in "Would you like to purchase a box of candy or a scented candle today?" I started working the following week after I had first contacted them. They picked me up on weekdays at 4:00 p.m., and we were done at 8:00 p.m., and on Saturdays, we would work from 9:00 a.m. to 5:00 p.m., which sometimes we would travel out of town. They would pick me up at my house along with other kids that were in my neighborhood. I would sell anywhere from ten to twenty items on weekdays, so I would end up making anywhere from ten to twenty dollars a day, and on Saturdays, I would sell between thirty to fifty items, so I would end up making thirty to fifty dollars. When you added this up for the week, I would make about $100 to $150 a week. This was pretty good for a twelve-year-old. They also took us on trips and outings. This was right on time for me. I could buy my own clothes and shoes for school, get my hair done, and have money for school lunch. I would not have to worry about people talking about me because I did not have the latest shoes or clothes. I was determined to buy them myself.

Your Gift Will Make Room for You

Ever since I was a young girl, I always had a gift for speaking with people. I was not shy; I was outspoken. When I used to go to my grandmother's shop on the South Side of Chicago, I was determined to help my grandmother sell some items. That was when she placed a table outside, and she put some items on the table for me to sell. I invited people to my table and was not timid about asking them to buy something off it, whether it was shampoo, conditioner, aloe vera juice, a kid's toy, or some lipstick. I had what people call the gift of gab. I loved to talk to people. My mother use to tell me when she used to go to my parent-teacher conferences that the teachers used to say, "She is a sweet little girl, but she likes to talk a lot."

When I joined the Elite Teens, when I look back, I was just walking in the gift that God had already given me. Selling candy door-to-door was no different than when I was six years old inviting strangers to my table in front of my grandmother's shop to buy something. This was no different than when I was four years old and my mother and father used to shout "Lady Ann!" and I would come running to serve them. I love to serve and help people. The Bible says in Proverbs 18:16 that your gift will make room for you. That is why I was able to be effective at selling for the Elite Teens. I loved talking to people, and I loved serving people what I think they should have.

God's Plans vs. Our Plans

I was twelve years old at the time, and we moved in the beginning of the summer. When schooltime rolled around, I was so nervous. I did not want to be the kid I was in Chicago—unpopular and unnoticed. This time was going to be different. This time, I was going to make a name for myself. I had a summer job at the time, which lasted throughout the school year, so I was able to buy my own brand-name clothes and shoes and get my hair done. I thought, *I am no longer going to be the odd one out. This is going to be different. I am going to be popular, by any means necessary.*

This part in my life was the beginning of God's plan for me. Not to say that it wouldn't be a rough road ahead, but this was God's plan of moving me out of Chicago into the place were, one day, I will be changed for His glory. At this particular time in my life, I was ready for any type of change. I felt that anything would be better than what I had already experienced. I was twelve years old at the time, and I didn't understand why I went through all I had went through. I do know now that it was necessary for me to move out of Chicago to Ohio for God to do a radical change in my life. At the time, I thought that it was just another unfortunate event because I had to leave my friends and all I knew to go to a foreign place and be all alone again. Now that I am changed in God, I wonder what would have happened if I stayed in Chicago. Would I have been changed in God like I am right now? Would I even be serving God like I am right now? Would I even be saved? In Jeremiah 29, God says, "I know the plans I have for you—plans not to harm you, plans to prosper you, and plans to bring you a hope and a future." This means that even though we cannot fully see what God is doing in our lives, He knows the ultimate plan for us. The enemy wants us to think when change happens in our lives, it will be miserable and not of God. He wants us fearful of moving forward. But we have to understand that if God allowed it to happen, then ultimately, it's of His purpose and a part of His divine plan.

Twists and Turns of Life

In the course life, we encountered many twists and turns. We experienced changes for the good and some changes for the bad. We experienced devastation, triumph, joy, excitement, progress, and setbacks. These life events and changes came to help you grow; they came to strengthen you. They were never intended to harm you. The enemy wants to use these to harm you, but when you are in God, they come to elevate you.

I hear many people ask, "Why did God allow negative things to happen in our lives?" Let me clarify that it's not God that caused negative things to happen in our lives. We have to understand that there is an enemy working against us, and through God's grace and mercy, He protects us even in negative situations. There are many roads that we may tread upon in this life—some smooth roads and some rocky roads. But the bottom line is it's still a road we must travel on until God gives us a different direction to take. When I think about it, by definition, the word *road* has two meanings. The first meaning is it is "a way or path leading from one place to another." The second meaning is it is "a series of events or a course of action that will lead to a particular outcome." Both definitions are needed throughout the course of our lives. The things or series of events will lead to a particular outcome called your life, and the outcomes that happen are based on your decision of what road you desire to take. Let's look at a road—you either can go straight, right, left, or backward. The decision of which road you will take is totally up to you. If you knew that danger was on a specific road, would you take that road? God gives us warning signs. What are the warning signs? It is when that little voice in your head tells you that you are not supposed to do this or you are not supposed to go there, but sometimes we ignore the little voice in our heads and head down that road anyway.

Broad Road, Narrow Road

I had a dream one night that shook me to the core. I was walking down a road. I was going at a very steady pace, but I was walking alone. Then I saw a person walking backward on the same road I was on. Then I saw another person who caught up with me, and then they just stopped and turned around and started heading back in the direction I just came from. Then I looked across, and I saw another road. There where thousands of people on this road. They looked like they were having a ball. They were waving their hands in the air. It looked like they were having a party, having fun. I started to become sad, and I wondered to myself, *Why am I on this road by myself?* Then I woke up. God immediately spoke to me and said, "Broad is the road that leads to destruction, and many find it, Narrow is the road that leads to everlasting life and only a few find it" This was a paraphrase found in Matt. 7:13–14. I started to weep. God gave me a prophecy in today's world. The Lord began giving me insight of my dream. The person who was walking backward was not walking toward the purpose that God had for them; they had a form of god, but operated in religion. They were not following the path of God. For the individual who had caught up with me but then turned around and started going back in the other direction, God gave me the revelation that this represented the people who were once walking in the path that God had for them, but they allowed issues and situations in their lives to cause them to turn around and go back the other way. For the individuals whom I saw across the way on another road having a good time, God showed me that they were people on the road to destruction—people who indulged in things of this world and people who did not have a love for God or did not even consider to be in relationship with God. So, my question to you is, what road are you going to take? The road that leads to destruction, or the road that leads to everlasting life? It seems like a simple answer. What is not so simple is when you have things of this world pulling you into a direction that is not of God, when temptation hits your life at one of your most vulnerable moments, and when you want to fit in like everyone else. This was my issue at a young age. I was soon to find out that by choosing that broad road, it almost cost me my life. But I thank God for His grace and mercy for keeping me throughout my foolish moments.

You have to make up your mind what you want to do. Do you want to do what others are doing and miss the plan of God for your life? Or do you dare to be different and walk in your peculiar attributes, which God has intended for you? You have many choices to get where you are trying to go. You can turn right or left. You might come to a fork in the road that forces you to make a decision on which way to go, and if you make a wrong turn, you might run into a dead end. Now you're backtracking, wasting time.

What I'm trying to say is that your road requires a course of action that will lead you to the intended result. You have to have your mind made up that you will choose the way of the Lord by any means necessary. God is trying to get us on a road of restoration back to Him. What does restoration mean? It is the process of returning something to their former place of condition. We were originally made in the image of God, according to His likeness (Gen. 1). Some things and events caused us to get off course, to go down the road that God did not intended for us to go. But once we acknowledge that God wants the best for us and He has a prosperous plan for our lives, it will be easy for us to accept the mistakes we had made and accept those things that had happened to us that were out of our control. Some changes in our lives come unexpectedly, but the question is, what are you going to do when that change comes? We have many choices we can make, but it is all about the right choice. We must adopt the mind-set that's found in Romans 8:28 (NIV): "And we know that in all things God works for the good of those who love him, who have been called according to his purpose." As long as we stay the course of the Lord, we will be just fine.

Chapter 6

Losing Who I Was Created to Be

For you created my inmost being; you knit me together in my mother's womb. I praise you because I am fearfully and wonderfully made; your works are wonderful, I know that full well.
—Ps. 139:13–14 NIV

When school started, I latched on to the first person that showed me any attention. That's all it took. I started hanging around with a group of people who introduced me to a world I did not even know existed. They introduced me to smoking weed, drinking alcohol, and smoking cigars. I wanted to fit in; I wanted to be noticed. Even though I knew it was wrong and I hated substance abuse and I was taught that it was wrong as a child, I did it anyway because I was determined to be popular. I was also introduced to being a whole new person doing things that was totally out of my character. I also found out quickly that if you are going to hang around a certain group of people, you cannot be scared of anything; and if one person fights in your circle, you all better fight or get talked about later. Soon after that, I got involved in a gang. I felt that they had my back; I felt that I was not that timid little nobody back in Chicago. I was coming into who I was meant to be.

I hated my name as a child and even as a teenager, so when I got into the gang, they changed my name from Rashieda to Chadie (pronounced "Shady"). I learned how to rap from my cousin; I got really good at it, and started rapping at parties and doing shows featuring local artists' albums. I was known in my neighborhood. Shortly after that, I got involved in menacing activities and started getting in trouble with the juvenile system. I did not care about it. I thought it was cool, and I was being noticed. Shortly after getting in trouble with the law for an incident that happened with a group of other kids, the police came to my grandmother's house looking for me. I jumped out the window and was gone from my home for about a week. My family was shocked about all that I was involved in, so my mother surprisingly came down to take me back to Chicago. I understood her concern, but I was no longer that little sweet girl she once knew. I had changed, and I was not going back to the old life I used to live. I was no longer rejected. I had friends—a lot of them—and I was not about to give up my popularity. I quickly thought of a plan and escaped out the back door without anyone even noticing. I was now labeled as a runaway and was on my own for about two months. I contacted my oldest sister, and she told me that my grandmother was concerned and all she wanted was for me to come home, so I did. I still did not change; I knew who I wanted to be—well, so I thought I did.

Lack of Self-Worth

In this stage in my life, I lacked self-worth. I changed my personality, my beliefs, and who I was just to be accepted by others. I did not even care if it was wrong; I was just tired of being the oddball in the bunch, and I was determined to fit in. Self-worth is our basis that sets the stage of who we are. If we think positive of ourselves, we would not allow things or people who come into our lives to think differently. When we operate with low self-worth, we allow the enemy to come in and bring people in our lives who will show us a glimpse of self-worth; meaning, they may stroke our ego to make us feel special, and as soon as they get what they want, they are gone. Lack of self-worth will have you doing things that are out of character just to feel better about yourself, even if it's just for a moment. The enemy is a trickster, and he is very crafty at coming in our lives when we feel most vulnerable, when we are weak, and when we are tired. I am not sure about you, but let me be transparent. Oftentimes, if I am weak or tired, I have the tendency to make poor decisions. The Bible says the enemy roams around like a lion, looking for who he can devour (1 Pet. 5:8). One of the attributes of a lion is that he is very patient; he will wait until a prey is weak, then he will strike. He is not fast at all. He tires his opponent out, then he goes in for the attack. This is why the enemy is compared to a lion—he has the same attributes. He is very patient; he waits until we are at a weak point in our lives, then he attacks. Let's use the example that Jesus gave us in Matthew 4:1–11 (NIV):

> Then Jesus was led by the Spirit into the wilderness to be tempted by the devil. After fasting forty days and forty nights, he was hungry. The tempter came to him and said, "If you are the Son of God, tell these stones to become bread."

> Jesus answered, "It is written: 'Man shall not live on bread alone, but on every word that comes from the mouth of God.'"

> Then the devil took him to the holy city and had him stand on the highest point of the temple. "If you are the Son of God," he said, "throw yourself down. For it is written: 'He will command his angels concerning you, and they will lift you up in their hands, so that you will not strike your foot against a stone.'"

> Jesus answered him, "It is also written: 'Do not put the Lord your God to the test.'"

> Again, the devil took him to a very high mountain and showed him all the kingdoms of the world and their

splendor. "All this I will give you," he said, "if you will bow down and worship me."

Jesus said to him, "Away from me, Satan! For it is written: 'Worship the Lord your God and serve him only.'"

Then the devil left him, and angels came and attended him.

This is the story where Jesus was fasting for forty days before He was to start the ministry that God had intended for Him. At the end of the forty days, He was tired and hungry. The devil came at a time when He was vulnerable in His flesh. The devil, being the trickster that he is, tried to get Jesus to forfeit the plan that Father God had for Him. He tried twisting the Holy Scriptures and tested Jesus's self-worth. But even though Jesus was weak in His flesh, He was still strong in the Spirit.

This is no different today. The enemy comes to test you when you are at your weakest point to try and get you to accept a false identity instead of walking in what God has called you to be. I dealt with this at a young age. Because of the negative events that had happened in my life, I was at a weak point, and this gave room for the devil, the tempter, to come and get me to accept an identity that was not created by God. Satan wanted me to take on his identity and attributes and stay far away from walking in the likeness of God and adapting God's attributes.

Our Self-Worth Is in the Image of God

Let's read Genesis 1:26–28 (NIV). It talks about who we were originally created to be and the power and authority we have.

Then God said, "Let us make mankind in our image, in our likeness, so that they may rule over the fish in the sea and the birds in the sky, over the livestock and all the wild animals, and over all the creatures that move along the ground."

So God created mankind in his own image, in the image of God, he created them; male and female he created them.

God blessed them and said to them, "Be fruitful and increase in number; fill the earth and subdue it. Rule over the fish in the sea and the birds in the sky and over every living creature that moves on the ground."

We were made in the image of God! This is why the enemy wants us to forfeit our God-given image and adapt his attributes. What are some of the attributes of God?

- God is eternal; we, too, have eternal life if we accept Jesus Christ (1 John 5:13).
- God is holy; we, too, are holy as we operate by the Holy Spirit (1 Pet. 1:16).
- God is unchanging; we, too, are unchanging if we follow Christ, His Word, and His commandments (Luke 9:23).
- God is all-powerful; we, too, are all-powerful by way of the Holy Spirit (Luke 10:19).
- God is creative; we, too, are creative. He has given us the mind to invent things (Exod. 35:35).
- God is wise; we are wise not in our own eyes but wise because God has given us wisdom through His Word (Exod. 35:31).
- God is love; we have the ability to love and be loved (Mark 12:30–31).
- God is merciful; it is our duty to show mercy to others, just as He has shown us mercy (Matt. 5:7).

The bottom line is that we are created in the image of God. We ought to be happy with the talents, gifts, and genetic makeup that He has given us. When we look in the mirror, if we are in Christ, we are looking at the very image of God. We need to stop focusing on what the world says how we should look and who we should be and start focusing on what God wants us to be.

You Are Fearfully and Wonderfully Made

Now let's look at Psalm 139:13–16 (NIV):

For you created my inmost being; you knit me together in my mother's womb.

I praise you because I am fearfully and wonderfully made; your works are wonderful; I know that full well.

My frame was not hidden from you when I was made in the secret place, when I was woven together in the depths of the earth.

Your eyes saw my unformed body; all the days ordained for me were written in your book before one of them came to be.

What do these scriptures mean? It says, "You created my most inner being." That means that the Almighty God has created you, and you were created in the image of God. Despite what people say, despite what you feel, and despite what society wants to label you as, you were created in the very image of our Creator.

It goes on to say, "You knit me together in my mother's womb." This means that before you were born God created you with purpose, He formed you. You were fearfully and wonderfully made. You were ordained to be here before you were even created. Anything that is contrary to this is a lie from the enemy. Oftentimes, we let things in our past, such as negative events, shape who we are, which could have been positive or negative in our lives.

I encouraged you today to jot down all the negative issues that happened in your life and put a check mark on the ones that are unresolved. And we pray and ask God to help you deal with those unresolved issues from your past hurt and failures because I am a firm believer that we can receive healing power of Jesus Christ. You do have a high self-worth in Jesus Christ because he made you in his very image!

Chapter 7

False Love

If you belonged to the world, it would love you as its own.
As it is, you do not belong to the world, but I have chosen
you out of the world. That is why the world hates you.
—John 15:19 NIV

By the age of fifteen, I got into a relationship. This relationship started off rocky, but it was something to pass the time, and I actually liked the person. He was a misfit like me, getting into trouble, so we hung out all the time. He started showing me attention, and I did not feel rejected like I did in the past from other relationships. One day, this person asked me when we were going to have sex; I was still a virgin at the time. I felt uncomfortable about this subject because it would always bring memories of when I was sexually assaulted as a child. I would make up some excuse or try to avoid it until, one day, I was given a choice—I either have sex or he was going to leave me. I felt those feelings of rejection rising up again, so I decided to have sex. Not long after, that person started being very controlling and being physically and mentally abusive. They did not want me to hang with my friends or family without him being present. If I said something he did not like, we would get into a big fight, and I would end up with a black eye and had to wear sunglasses to cover it up. I'm not saying every day was bad in this relationship; I did have good times, but honestly, did I know what good was? I knew for sure when the bad times happened—not all the time—but when it happened, it was bad. *Really* bad.

One day, I was in the store, and this guy came up to me and said, "Sweetie, you are too beautiful to be wearing those glasses, who is hitting you?" I felt a big lump in my throat. I could not speak. It was then I realized and asked myself, *Am I really trapped in an abusive relationship?* I walked out without saying a word to the nice-looking young man—I felt so embarrassed. The abusive situation had gotten so bad my friend felt that if I did decide to leave the relationship, he might kill me. I started to wonder myself that it might actually happen if I did.

I had my first child at the age of seventeen. I hid my pregnancy from my family until I was about seven months along. I was very slender, and it was the winter months, so I always wore a coat to hide my pregnancy. I was very clever—so I thought. When I was about two months along, I started going to the neighborhood clinic to receive prenatal care. I can remember during my first visit, they sent a case manager in to discuss my options. This tall, slender lady with short dark hair came in to speak to me about my options. She looked at me and said, "Honey, you know you can have an abortion. You still have your whole life ahead of you." I was so disturbed by the statement. I kindly told her, "I am sorry, ma'am, but I do not believe in abortions. It was my choice to have unprotected sex, so it is not the baby's fault to die because of my mistake." She looked at me with such a puzzled look, maybe it was because she was not expecting for me to give this answer—well, someone who was a young girl of sixteen.

I continued receiving prenatal care and catching buses to my scheduled appointment, my boyfriend tagging along. One day, I had to catch the bus by myself. I was about six months along in my pregnancy. I felt the baby moving all around; the movement brought me so much joy. I thought, *Wow, before I became pregnant, I did not care if I lived or died, and now here is a baby who would need to be cared for by me. I had a reason to live now.* I looked at my belly and said to him, "I will not let anything happen to you. You will not live the life that I did growing up, and you will never go through what I did." Tears started to roll down my cold cheeks. I quickly wiped them away; the bus was coming down the street. *It is time to handle my business,* I thought. No more living for myself; I had someone depending on me to make it in this weary world.

After my appointment, I found out that my family received word that I was pregnant. I had told my sister a couple of months ago, in which she told my cousin, and the cat was out the bag then. I acted like I was upset with my cousin when, in all actuality, I was relieved. I was tired of hiding it for so long. My mother and grandmother were upset, but they soon accepted the fact that they were going to have another grandchild or great-grandchild. The baby was born, and he was the most beautiful baby I had ever seen. I fell in love—love at first sight. Three years later, I had a second child, and it was love all over again.

At one point throughout my time of dating and relationships, I found out that one person I was in a relationship with had a problem with substance abuse. They would steal from our household, other people, businesses, or whoever to support the habit. The person I was in a relationship with at the time ended up in prison, and I started having a sense of freedom. I wasn't being controlled because they were in jail. I started going to the nightclubs with my friends. I was twenty years old, and I was enjoying myself. While I was having the time of my life, I thought, *I did not need to be with this person who is always so controlling.* But the truth was when they got out, I was right back in the relationship, and the feeling of being depressed set in all over again. All the letters and the phone calls I received while he was in jail about how he had changed for the better turned out to be nothing more than lies. He was still physically and mentally abusive. I felt trapped, and I had to get out!

One day, this person took my car and was gone for about three days. I did not know where this person was. I called all our friends, the jail, and any place I thought one could be at, but I had no luck. Then he finally arrived home. When I looked outside, I saw all four of the windows in my car, which I worked hundreds of hours to get, were busted. I yelled and screamed, "What did you do!" We got into a big fight. This person slammed me to the ground, and my body just shook.

I laid there, thinking, *Why am I going through this?* The person soon fell asleep; I could tell he was intoxicated. Then it happened. I mustered up enough nerve to leave him. I left while he was asleep. I left all our belongings and left the house that I helped create. I cleaned out all the glass scattered on the seats and the floor of the car. I put garbage bags over the windows. I wrapped my kids up in extra clothes and blankets (it was the dead of winter), and I packed up the kids and moved in with my grandmother. I had thoughts of taking him back, but as soon as I did, we got into the worst fight ever, and this person winded up going to jail, and that was the end of that.

About a month later, I started dating a friend I knew from my teen years. The relationship lasted long enough for me to get pregnant with my daughter, and it ended soon due to my psychological issues and their issues combined. I was back to square one. I went to the club and drank regularly to hide the pain I was feeling. I was single with three kids. I felt alone, I felt rejected, I felt empty, I felt angry, I felt bitter, and I felt unhappy. Was this the plan for my life? Was I cursed with bad relationships? I thought I was meant for something greater, but all that I had experienced at this point was heartache and pain. What happened to the little girl who thought she could change the world? What happened to the little girl who wanted to help everyone? What happened? Why am I even here?

Hitting Rock Bottom

The rejection, the hurt, the pain, and the bad experiences I had encountered up until this point in my life left room for the enemy to come in and bring a false sense of love in my life. I was always a daddy's girl, and when my parents divorced, it was like my father divorced us. I would not see him unless it was on our own accord to try and reach out to him. This, combined with rejection from my childhood, created the perfect way for the enemy to bring in someone who would look like they were the one to show me love, but in all actuality, it was the total opposite. I don't blame the people in my past for what I went through in our so-called relationship, for the mere fact they had issues that stemmed from childhood as well. This had happened in their lives as well, which was out of their control, so the enemy was also coming into their space of brokenness to cause them to do things contrary to the will of God.

I had reached a state of brokenness, and this was the place where depression and suicide dwelled. This was a dangerous place. I thank God for His grace and mercy over my life because I could have reached a place where I was ready to give up on life. One thing that helped me were my kids. I had to live for them. The enemy would try and put thoughts in my mind as I was driving, saying, "Just run off the cliff." I used to think those were my thoughts, but when I came into the knowledge of Christ, I knew those thoughts were never my own. It was from the enemy to try and get me to forfeit the plan of God on my life. He tried to tempt Jesus with the same thing when He was at a weak point. Matthew 4:5–7 (NIV) says, "Then the devil took him [Jesus] to the holy city and had him stand on the highest point of the temple. 'If you are the Son of God,' he said, 'throw yourself down. For it is written: "He will command his angels concerning you, and they will lift you up in their hands, so that you will not strike your foot against a stone."' Jesus answered him, "It is also written: 'Do not put the Lord your God to the test.'"

The devil was trying to get Jesus to abort the mission and purpose that Jesus came to do—show the way to live and die for our sins. This would never happen if He had listened to the devil. This is no different than the tactic the devil is using on us today. He wants us to forfeit the plan of God over our lives.

Brokenness Is a Dark Place

When you are in the stage of brokenness, you feel hopeless, you feel like giving up, and depression kicks in. You find yourself crying at any moment and do not know why. You can be in a crowd full of people and still feel alone. You feel like separating yourself; and you don't feel like praying, you don't feel like fasting, and you don't feel like reading your Bible. You're in a place where everything and everybody seems to be getting on your nerves. You're frustrated, and you might even be on the verge of cussing folks out. Then your physical body starts to react in this stage; and you start having aches, pains, headaches, heartaches, stress, and fatigue. In this stage, you start to doubt God. This brokenness could literally kill you spiritually, mentally, and physically. These emotions can rise out of nowhere, but even though these feelings arise, the key is you cannot stay in this state.

The Bible talks about one of God's servants whose name is Abraham. Even though Abraham was faced with a hopeless situation, he still believed in God and the promise that God had told him. The Bible states in Romans 4:18–19 (NIV) that "against all hope, Abraham in hope believed and so became the father of many nations, just as it had been said to him, 'So shall your offspring be.' Without weakening in his faith, he faced the fact that his body was as good as dead—since he was about a hundred years old—and that Sarah's womb was also dead." So no matter what the situation is, no matter how low you think you have fallen, God is able and capable to turn the situation around. The enemy wants us to stay in a hopeless state. The enemy does not want us to come out of our situation; he wants us to think that we cannot rise from the depths of despair. I am here to tell you *can* and you *will*! I am a living witness that God can change things around for your good in an instant.

Chapter 8

The Transformation

*Therefore, if anyone is in Christ, the new creation
has come: The old has gone, the new is here!*
—2 Cor. 5:17 NIV

One day, I was talking on the phone with my oldest sister, and I was telling her how I was feeling at the time. I remember telling her that I felt empty inside, I felt that I was trying to drink all the water in the world but was still thirsty—not even knowing that what I was feeling was the solution that Jesus gave to the woman at the well when He told her, "Whoever drink of this water will never thirst again" (John 4:14 NIV). I went on to say that "I have friends, a social life, I'm in school, but I still feel empty inside." She said in a calm voice, "Maybe it's because you need God." I pondered on this thought, but not for long. I thought, *Maybe so.*

A few months later, my aunt invited me to her church. I was so amazed with the preacher. It seemed like everything he was saying across the pulpit was directed toward me. I started to wonder if my aunt told him about me and what I was dealing with. Every time I came into the church, it was like God was speaking directly to me, so I kept coming, even if I had gone to the bar the night before. I would arrive at church right in time for the preaching to start. One day, I prayed to

God and said, "God, I am tired of living this way. I don't understand the Bible when I try to read it. If you want me to learn your ways, help me to understand. When I start to read the Bible at the beginning, in the book of Genesis, I lose interest when I get to the book of Leviticus." This was when I heard God speak to me for the very first time. He told me to start in the book of Matthew. I started to read the book of Matthew, and I was in shock. Everything I was reading was crystal clear. Everything I was dealing with at the time was right there in black and white! Even though I was reading and understanding the Bible, I still struggled with going out to the clubs and drinking, so I asked God, "Please take the taste of things that displeases you out of my mouth." Soon after I petitioned my request to Him, He started removing negative people and things out of my life. When I went to take a sip of alcohol, my stomach hurt so bad that I did not touch it again. I started getting involved with my church. Then one day, after service, I was asked to be on the praise-and-worship team. I told them I didn't sing; I rapped. And the thought of me singing was absurd to me, but when I opened my mouth, the glory of God filled the place. I did not have a clue that I possessed this powerful gift.

Things were going well. It seemed as if I was transforming into someone who was always there but was not coming out because she was locked away in a far-off place. The change felt so natural. I was coming into who I was meant to be, and then it happened.

The Negative Seed Had Sprouted and Made Its Roots

One day, I was over a family member's house, and I heard the name of my childhood assaulter. He was in the house! I thought, *My god, is he really here!* I froze in crippling fear. I felt sick to my stomach, and I felt like crying and fighting at the same time. My friend, who was not saved, knew what had happened to me. She quickly said, "You want me to call my brother? We can have him beat up." Now if I had not changed in the Lord, this might have been my first choice. I told her, no, that it was not necessary. I just wanted to go home. I quickly got out of there.

I went home and cried to the Lord, "Why now, God, why now? I have been in this town ever since I was twelve years old. I'm twenty-five and never heard this person's name, let alone saw him!"

I instantly started praying. I felt the peace of God, and under the guidance of the Holy Spirit, I started praying for my perpetrator, then I forgave him. I could not believe what had just happened. *Did I just really pray for and forgive the person who robbed me of my innocence and who caused the very first negative seed and stronghold to take root in my life? Why is this happening now, Lord? What is this all about?* Then I heard the Lord say, "I had to bring what was deep down rooted in you so you can be healed because I have something that you need to do." Then He told me to write down everything I had been through. *I pulled out a piece of paper and started listing, and on that list were* substance abuse; physical, verbal, and mental abuse; rejection; teen pregnancy; sexual assault as a child; being in a gang; engaging in menacing activities; going to juvenile jail; and the list went on and on. When I was done writing down all the things I had experienced, there were twenty-three negative situations I had been through by the age of twenty. Then the Lord said, "Now this is your ministry." I started crying and said yes to the Lord that day and was healed from things of my past.

The Beginning of the End

I had a clear understanding that now I must serve God wholeheartedly. I knew I must give up the lifestyle that I once lived because it was contrary to what God wanted for my life. I had to change my way of thinking, to line up with the Word and will of God. God makes it clear in the Word that our flesh—worldly ways—cannot please God. Let's look at some scriptures that talk about dealing with our flesh to get a deeper understanding. In order to rid ourselves of our fleshly ways and desires, we need to know and speak the scriptures over our lives.

> The mind governed by the flesh is hostile to God; it does
> not submit to God's law, nor can it do so. (Rom. 8:7 NIV)

I have been crucified with Christ. It is no longer I who live, but Christ who lives in me. And the life I now live in the flesh I live by faith in the Son of God, who loved me and gave himself for me. (Gal. 2:20 NIV)

But I say, walk by the Spirit, and you will not gratify the desires of the flesh. (Gal. 5:16 NIV)

Put to death therefore what is earthly in you: sexual immorality, impurity, passion, evil desire, and covetousness, which is idolatry. (Col. 3:5 NIV)

For the desires of the flesh are against the Spirit, and the desires of the Spirit are against the flesh, for these are opposed to each other, to keep you from doing the things you want to do. (Gal. 5:17 NIV)

There are many scriptures in the Bible that talk about the flesh, but these are just a few you can meditate on that can help you override the flesh.

When I found Christ, this was the beginning of the end. What does that mean? It means that it was the end of me living for myself and was the beginning of me living for God. So what did I do first? I started getting in my Word. What is the Word? It is the Bible. Instead of me reading it like a book, I asked the Lord where he wanted me to start. He told me to start in the book of Matthew. I started reading it, and it seemed that everything I was going through at the time, the book of Matthew was addressing the situation and giving me instructions, love, peace, and hope. I was hanging around with people who had a love for God like me. I started to go to Christian concerts, events, programs, and conferences. I had a deep hunger for God, and I wanted to be more like Him. I felt great. I was happy that things where turning around. I was growing in God, but on the flip side, there was the enemy. He did not want me to change. Why do I say this? It's because it seemed like random things were happening to try and cause me to go back to my fleshly ways.

I Don't Want to Let You Go

One night, my sister and I came home from an album-release Christian concert. We really got into the presence of God and left the concert feeling rejuvenated and empowered. As soon as I parked my car in front of my sister's house, I started to smell smoke in the car. We quickly exited the vehicle. Then I saw where the smoke was coming from. It was coming from under the hood of the car. I opened the hood of the car and saw that one of the parts was on fire. I quickly got a towel from the trunk of the car and eliminated the flames coming from the part. I looked at my sister, and we both had a knowing that the enemy did not want us to continue in the joy we were experiencing after we left the Christian concert. I thought, *Wow, what a way to end the day.* This was the first of many things that was trying to come up against me as I was trying to break away from my old life and follow God. Why am I telling you this? Why do I feel it is important to mention in this book? It is to let you know that if you are at the point where you want to change your old life and follow after God, the enemy will try his best to keep you from following God and to revert you to your old way of thinking or to make you just leave God altogether. For those who are already in God, just know that the enemy will also try his best to make you leave God as well. He will try and cause events to happen for you to be so discouraged that you will throw in the towel. Just to be transparent, the devil tried everything he could to try and cause me to leave my new life in God and to go back to my old life, in which God was not at the top of my list. Even through all the temptations, setbacks, and failures, I kept pressing through because I knew God was going to work all of it out for my good.

Let's look at God's servant in the Bible who went by the name of Job. The devil was plotting to cause Job to leave God. He actually went to God and was confident that Job would curse God and not follow him at all.

> Then the Lord said to Satan, "Have you considered my servant Job? There is no one on earth like him; he is blameless and upright, a man who fears God and shuns evil."

"Does Job fear God for nothing?" Satan replied. "Have
you not put a hedge around him and his household
and everything he has? You have blessed the work
of his hands, so that his flocks and herds are spread
throughout the land. But now stretch out your hand
and strike everything he has, and he will surely curse
you to your face."

The Lord said to Satan, "Very well, then, everything he
has is in your power, but on the man, himself do not lay
a finger." Then Satan went out from the presence of the
Lord. (Job 1:8–12 NIV)

If you follow the story of Job, you will know the devil tried to
cause Job to curse God and die. He lost his family, his finances, and
his health; and these almost caused him to question his own identity
in God. This is no different today; the devil will try and cause havoc
to come in your life to get you to turn away from God, but rest assured
God has faith that you will prevail. After all Job went though, God
gave Job double what he had lost for his trouble. To be transparent,
when I decided to leave my old life and follow after God, I lost friends.
Things that I did for entertainment, I no longer did; places I used to
go, I did not go anymore. Even though I lost those things, God replaced
them with a whole new abundant life that would bring me fulfillment.
He placed people in my life who were going the same path as me. He
gave me ministry gifts that I never knew I had. He gave me more than
double, and it was more than what I could have ever imagined.

Transformation Started from the Very Beginning

Since the creation of man and woman, we have been dealing with
continual transformation. In Genesis, God told Adam and Eve not to
eat from the tree that was in the middle of the garden or they will die.
Satan came in and, with his deception, told them the total opposite of

what God had said—that they will not die if they eat from the tree in
the middle of the garden. So this situation caused the first negative seed
to be planted in the minds of the first humans, Adam and Eve. From
the very beginning, the negative seed went against what God had said.
This was the very first stronghold that was set up in the minds of the
first man and woman. Just like God planted seeds in us that bear good
fruits such as love, joy, peace, kindness, and goodness (Gal. 5:22–23),
the enemy can try and plant negative seeds that are contrary to God
(Matt. 13:38–39).

That's why it is so important to kill the negative seeds, roots, and
things planted by the enemy in our lives. This is why we have to have
a new transformation when we come in Christ, to give up the old
person who we thought we were. In the book of John chapter 3, Jesus
was telling a Jewish leader that no one can see the kingdom of God
unless he is born again. What does this mean? You see, when we came
in this world, we were first born of water; meaning, we came from our
mother's womb. We carry the sins of past generations, even from the
disobedience of the first man and woman, Adam and Eve. We have
those negative seeds that have been passed down from generation to
generation, and then we grow and accumulate our own negative seeds,
which in turn transform into strongholds.

It is imperative that we accept Jesus Christ as our Lord and Savior
when we put off the old person. This is what Jesus was talking about
when He said we must be born again. We are born again in the Spirit,
adopting a life that mimics Christ. We encounter a whole new life that
is contrary to the one we once knew. Second Corinthians 5:17 (NIV)
says, "Therefore, if anyone is in Christ, the new creation has come: The
old has gone, the new is here!" When we accept Jesus as our Lord and
Savior, we have to start changing the way we think. We have to change
the way we live. We must get rid of hold habits that do not line up with
the Word of God. We have to allow our thinking to be changed by the
Word of God.

Let's think of it this way: Think of our minds as a computer, and
we have received miscommunications, junk mails, and even acquired
some viruses. We now have to clean or reboot the computer to its

pre-purchased state. Then it's time to install new programs that are going to be beneficial to the computer's well-being, such as an antivirus software. This is no difference than you and I. We had an original state as humans before the fall—meaning, until the sin of Adam and Eve was released into the earth, which we must get back to. This is where Jesus comes into play. Because God so love the world, He gave His only begotten Son so we can be saved (John 3:16). God wants us to get back to our original state. This is why Jesus died for us. So in order for us to live again, we must die. What do I mean? This means the old person must die, and we must adopt the new one through the redemption of Jesus Christ! We can take the example of a computer; it is important to install an antivirus to avoid potential problems from damaging the computer's hard drive. The antivirus for our soul is the Holy Bible and it helps to protect us from potential harm.

How can we transform to who God wants us to be? How can we transform when we have learned information that has been embedded into our soul, our very being, since the beginning of time? This is found in Romans 12. Romans 12:2 (NIV) says the following:

> Do not conform to the pattern of this world but be transformed by the renewing of your mind. Then you will be able to test and approve what God's will is—his good, pleasing and perfect will.

This gives us the answer to how we can be transformed into who God want us to be. We have to get rid of the old thinking that does not line up with the will or Word of God, and we need to have our minds transformed by the Holy Scripture. We can no longer go by the world standards; we have to be in alignment with God standards. We need to have a virus protection in our minds, and the virus protection is the Bible, and just like we have to renew our spyware protection, we have to continue to renew our minds with the Bible. We cannot just read it sparingly; we need to read and study on a continual basis so we are prepared when an issue comes our way. I had a computer once, and I allowed the antivirus protection expire. I did not renew it. As a result of letting the antivirus protection expire, I ended up getting viruses on my computer, and it took more money to get the viruses off my computer than if I had not let the antivirus software expire. If I had the protection it needed, it would have blocked the viruses. Let's look at this as if the Bible were our protection—if we do not read it and put the words into our minds, we will not have the protection we need to block out the viruses sent by the enemy. Our minds should be so filled with God's Word that it will automatically block the negative thinking that tries to come our way. This also helps build positive self-efficacy.

Upgrading Your Self-Efficacy

It is mentioned that people with low or weak self-efficacy have the following traits: they avoid challenging tasks, they believe that difficult tasks are beyond their capabilities, they focus on personal failure and negative outcomes, and they lose confidence easily.

We have to go to another level in our self-efficacy. I want to just talk for a moment about the word *self-efficacy*. First, we need to know what this word means. *Self-efficacy* is a word used widely among psychologists and philosophers in today's era. One psychologist by the name of Albert Bandura has defined this word as "belief in one's ability to succeed in specific situations, how one judges one's own competence to complete tasks and reach goals." It comes from the root word *efficacy*, which is the power to produce an effect. So when you add the word *self* in front of *efficacy*, it means the self's ability to produce an effect. You can have a low level or a high level of self-efficacy. In order to transform into who God has called you to be, in addition of removing the negative things that has been planted over the years, one would have to believe that they can change.

Levels of self-efficacy is developed early in life, in childhood, as we deal with all types of experiences, tasks, and situations, which continue to mold us as we go through this situation called life. Having low or negative self-efficacy is just another tactic of the enemy to get us to doubt our God-given abilities to be and do what God is calling us to do. Having a weak self-efficacy will cause one not to believe they can overcome forms of addiction reach their dreams and goals, prosper, change bad habits, or change their way of thinking. One way we can develop low self-efficacy is through our negative emotions. Fear, sadness, disappointments, and failures are some ways the enemy can move throughout our lives; and we will block ourselves from reaching our goals and our destiny.

Misconceptions of Fear

I want to talk about the emotion fear. God had told me at a very pivotal point in my life that I must scratch everything I once knew to adopt the new. This means I must put aside my old way of thinking if He was going to give me fresh revelation that would direct my path. What does this mean? The Bible tells us in Mark 2:22 (NIV) that "no one pours new wine into old wineskins. Otherwise, the wine will burst the skins, and both the wine and the wineskins will be ruined. No, they pour new wine into new wineskins." This means that if you have an old way of thinking, if God gives you a new way of perceiving something or doing something, you will not receive it because you are too busy focusing on the old way. This is why God told me to scratch everything I thought I knew so I could embrace the new things He was going to give me. This is not to say that you have to really hit the Delete button on all you have learned up until now, but you must have an open mind that God can do things a different way to get His work done in us or in the earth. The Bible says, "'For my thoughts are not your thoughts, neither are your ways my ways,' declares the LORD" (Isa. 55:8 NIV).

The Lord began to show me misconceptions that has been a part of me for many years. One was fear. Now I don't know about you, but I grew up thinking that a little bit of fear was okay. Many psychologists have said that a small amount of fear is good for you. It helps with focus; it helps you be more aware, but God showed me that if this small amount of fear continues to be activated in your life, it has the potential to turn into a full-blown phobia. What is a phobia? By definition, a *phobia* is an "extreme or irrational fear or aversion to something." There are different types of phobias: Situational—meaning that a situation has happened in your life that made you have a fearful attitude toward it. Animal phobias mean you are scared of certain animals; literary phobias mean you to have a fear of books, writing, and even speaking in public. Having an environmental phobia means one is scared of the rain, thunderstorms, tornadoes, and so forth.

Most of us have dealt with situational phobias, which means an event has happened in our lives to make us be fearful. Just to be transparent, because of what happened to me as a child, being sexually assaulted, it caused me to be afraid of relationships that required intimacy. Also, because of the constant rejection I faced caused me to be what I call a people pleaser, which is someone who, despite how it makes you feel, will do whatever necessary to make another person happy. It does not matter if I was not happy as long as that other person was happy. This is an unhealthy situation to be in. This leads to people manipulating the individual who is doing the people-pleasing. This also evokes fear of losing relationships if they do not do things to please another person.

Negative Effects of Fear

I am in the medical field, and I do a lot of research on the physical effects of the body and how emotions affect the mind. What I found out about the effects of fear was astonishing. Fear can affect your entire being. It can affect your physical state, and it can also affect your immune system. The immune system is an important mechanism in your body that fights off infection. When a virus or bacteria enters the body, the immune system reacts and sends what are called white bloods cells to fight off the infection. If one's immune system is down, it cannot fight off diseases and illnesses like it should. This can cause one to become sick or have prolonged sicknesses because the immune system is not fighting off the infection.

I have researched that the effects of fear can weaken the immune system, which predisposes you to illness and diseases. Prolonged fear can also cause heart problems, stomach problems such as ulcers, decreased fertility, accelerated aging, and even premature death. So if you are experiencing any of these issues, perform a self-check! Ask yourself, "Am I always fearful?" So, my question to those who proclaim a little fear is good is, if it's so good, then why does it lead to many health problems?

Fear Affects the Mind

Continual or prolonged fear can also lead to things that can impair the mind. It can impair the formation of long-term memories, it can impair emotions, it can cause one to become anxious all the time, and it can affect decision-making, causing one to be impulsive. It can lead to fatigue, depression, and PTSD (post-traumatic stress disorder); and it can also lead to brain damage. So, I ask again, how can fear be good? If you have been mentally clouded, ask yourself, "Have I've been operating in fear?" You might be saying to yourself, "I am not fearful of anything. I don't have any phobias," but there is one fear that many people don't even realize we are operating in, and it is called the fear of the unknown. Most of us want the plan for our life laid out in front of us. We want to know the next steps to our destiny. When we get into situations and circumstances that are out of our control, we want to know the end result or we become fearful of the outcome. This fear of the unknown can plague us and rob us from the peace that God wants us to have.

Giving It Over to God

How can we walk in peace and not fear of the unknown? It's found in 1 Peter 5:7 (NIV): "Cast all your anxiety on him because he cares for you." It's also found in Philippians 4:6–7 (NIV): "Do not be anxious about anything, but in every situation, by prayer and petition, with thanksgiving, present your requests to God. And the peace of God, which transcends all understanding, will guard your hearts and your minds in Christ Jesus." This is how we can walk in peace and not in fear. We have to pray and give it over to God. One of my mottoes in life is if you cannot do anything about it, why worry about it? If I cannot physically fix the problem, it's easier for me to just let God handle it. He will do a better job of dealing with the situation than I would have. Matthew 11:28–30 gives us great advice when we feel like we are at our lowest point in life, when we feel like the world is on our shoulders, and when we feel like we cannot take another adverse event in our already hectic lives. Jesus tells us in Matthew 11:28–30 (NIV) the following:

> Come to me, all you who are weary and burdened, and I will give you rest. Take my yoke upon you and learn from me, for I am gentle and humble in heart, and you will find rest for your souls. For my yoke is easy and my burden is light.

Why did Jesus use the phrase "take my yoke upon you"? Well, what is a yoke? A yoke is a wooden beam normally used between a pair of oxen or other animals to enable them to pull together a load when working in pairs. The Lord gave me this interpretation. If we take Jesus's yolk, He is able to pull us together when we feel like we are falling apart. He is able direct and guide us where we should go. When we have a load that is unbearable for us, Jesus understands, and He will take care of everything. The heavy load will not be heavy anymore. It will be light, and we just traded the heavy load to receive the lightweight of God's peace, comfort, and serenity. If I knew this years ago, I would have handed over all my issues to obtain the peace of God!

The Lord began to speak to me about this little fear that many people have said is good for you. God directed me to 2 Timothy 1:7 (NKJV), and it says, "For God has not given us a spirit of fear, but of power and of love and of a sound mind."

After reading this scripture, God then asked me this question, "If I did not give you the spirit of fear, who then gave it to you?" My mind was blown away. He was so right. If God did not give fear, then it must be from the enemy. Since my early stages of life, fear has come into my life someway, somehow. Fear unleashes an unpleasant feeling. My stomach starts to hurt, my heart races, I feel nauseated, I cannot think clear, and it causes me to be anxious. If God intended for me to have peace, then surely He did not want me to fear this way? You have heard in Proverbs 9:10 that "the fear of the Lord is the beginning of wisdom" (NIV). This is not the fear that causes you to be impaired; the fear of God refers to a specific sense of respect, awe, and submission. This is reverence unto God.

No Need to Fear; You Have Power

Luke 10:19 (NIV) says, "I have given you authority to trample on snakes and scorpions and to overcome all the power of the enemy; nothing will harm you." This means no matter what will try to come your way, God has given you the power to overcome it! You are much stronger than you think! With this type of power, you can walk in the confidence that God is with you during your transformation, during your hard times, and during your low moments. You are made in the image of God. You have power to command the space you occupy to line up with the will and plan of God! You can do it; you just need to raise your level of self-efficacy. You can and you will be what God has called you to be!

You Were Made in the Image of God

In Genesis 1, God said, "Let us make man in our own image, according to our likeness, and let them have dominion over everything." So if we were made in the image of God, we have so many of His attributes. We are creative, prosperous, wise, holy, righteous, powerful, loving, strong, and the list goes on. If we are made in the image of God and have all these attributes, then why in the world are we living beneath our potential? We have to declare and decree the Word of God over our lives and stop waiting on someone else to give us affirmation. I pose this question to you: How do you know who you are if you don't

know who you are? In other words, how do you know and move in the
attributes of God if you do not study the Word or spend time with Him
to get to know Him? This is why we need to stay in the Holy Scripture.
We have to cast down the old way of thinking, those strongholds that
have been occupying minds, and replace that empty space with the
Word of God. This is a continual thing we must do as we go through
life and situations that develop into a stronghold in our minds. The
scripture says that we are transformed by the renewing of our minds.
To renew is to change, refresh, and if you put "ing" on the end of *renew*,
this means this has to be done on a continual basis. It does not matter
if you been in church for twenty year or twenty minutes—we have to
continue to renew our minds with the Word of God. This will build a
strong self-efficacy.

Attributes of a Positive Self-Efficacy

Having a positive self-efficacy empowers you to walk in confidence
of who you are and move in the purpose and plan that God has called
you to do. When we have a strong or positive self-efficacy, we carry
these positive traits:

- We view challenging problems as tasks to be mastered.
- We form a stronger sense of commitment to our interests.
- We have the ability to recover quickly from setbacks and
  disappointments.
- We have a sense of purpose and are eager to accomplish goals
  and fulfill dreams.

We have a positive self-efficacy achieved by knowing who we are
in Christ, being transformed by the renewing of our minds by tearing
down strongholds that have been built up overtime through challenges,
experiences, and disappointments. This is also achieved by feeding our
minds with the Word of God on a continual basis, which will block negative
thinking from coming in to corrupt our perception of who we are in God.

Chapter 9

The Victory

But you are a chosen people, a royal priesthood, a holy nation,
God's special possession, that you may declare the praises of him
who called you out of darkness into his wonderful light.

—1 Pet. 2:9 NIV

Victory through Obedience

When I decided to follow the Lord, He kept showing parts of my
destiny. He started to direct my steps in what I needed to do. One day, I
was riding with my friend, and the Lord spoke to me, "Start a Christian
women's group." I was so amazed at the audible voice that spoke in
my ear. It was like what the Bible calls a still, small voice (1 Kings
19:11–13). I told my friend what I just heard. She was in agreement of
starting a women's group. I thought, *What would this women's group be
like?* I never started a women's group, but I wanted to be obedient to
God and what He had called me to do.

My friend and I started to think of a name. My concept was that
women should be more united than what they were right now. Then
it came through my friend, and she said, "You should call it United
Sisters." It was like a light bulb went off. It had a ring to it. It had
meaning. We were all sisters in Christ, and we must be united for a

greater purpose in God. When I got home, I started working on the mission statement, the purpose, and plans to start the first meeting. I wanted to start right away; I wanted to be obedient to the Lord.

United Sisters (Women Inspiring Women)

For the first meeting, I asked a friend of mine who I worked with if she would lead the meeting. She was a pastor's wife, and she often taught at her church. I invited people I knew to come to my house for what was like a Bible study, but we also had discussions. I served light refreshments. This was viewed by the people who attended as a relaxing atmosphere because the meeting was not in the setting of a traditional church or building.

I started this women's group in November of 2006. Many testimonies came out of this women's group. We went on trips to see well-known speakers, went to the movies to see Christian films when it came out, had outreach events for the community, and had weekly meetings to discuss different topics out of the Bible. I met so many people throughout the course of United Sisters. I was even able to have a known prostitute, who lived across the street from me, come to the women's group, and she broke down in tears as she received healing for her soul at that meeting. No one judged anyone, and we always said that if anyone shared any confidential information, it would go no further than the room we occupied.

Through United Sisters, the Lord also instructed me to create a program called Eliminating Burdens & Barriers, in which I did a four-week program at the local women's shelter. This program was created to help individuals identify barriers that were holding them back from becoming successful and to create interventions to remove those burdens in their lives. It was uplifting, as I had different speakers come in and teach on different topics, while also inspiring the participants to be and do better. At the end of the fourth week, I cooked dinner for the ladies at the shelter and gave them a certificate of completion. This was an emotional moment. The ladies cried as they went around the room, saying how they were grateful for me coming. Then one young lady, I would never forget, started to speak. She was twenty-one years old, and she was in school to obtain another degree when she lost her job. She stated that she did not want to stay at her aunt's house because she did not want to be a burden to her, so she chose to come to the shelter. She began to say to me that she could not believe someone took the time to create a program to help and inspire them without getting paid, without being recognized or noticed, but just did it because they cared. She began to thank me. I don't think there was a dry eye in the room. I told them that I knew I came to help them, but they were helping me as well—helping me to be more like Christ in my words and deeds.

Throughout the course of United Sisters (Women Inspiring Women), the Lord gave me victory through my obedience. It deepened my relationship with God and gave me a deeper understanding being a servant of God. It also helped me go deeper in studying the Bible and gaining knowledge and wisdom as I studied different topics. I got the victory because, through this avenue, God elevated me spiritually.

One day, after the women's group meeting, I went into my bathroom and I just started feeling sad. At this time, I was single with three young children, and I was not receiving any support physically or financially from the fathers. It weighed heavy on me. I started to cry and asked God, "Why do I have to take care of these kids by myself? Other people who are not with their kid's fathers at least got financial help from the absent parent." Then I heard the Lord say so softly, "But I graced you to do it." Then He started reminding me how blessed I was. I had a four-bedroom house, and my bills were manageable. I had a car, food, and clothes, and my kids did not want for anything. I started to cry even more and thanked God how blessed I really was.

Forty Days and Forty Nights

The Lord was doing quick work in my transformation. I had a hunger for the things of the Lord. I was involved in church; I was conducting the women's group. I was what they called sold-out for

Christ. I was not doing the things I used to do in my past. God was changing me and changing me fast.

One day, in prayer, I heard the Lord say, "You need to fast." I thought, *I don't have a clue about fasting. I have never done it before.* One thing I did know was that I trusted God. I said to myself, *If He told me to fast, then He would give me the instructions.* So I waited to hear clear instructions. I started seeing the number 40 everywhere. I kept hearing the number 40 everywhere. It was obvious at this point that I would be fasting for forty days. Then I heard the Lord say, "Forty days liquids only." I was shocked. I thought, *Is there such a thing?* I told my aunt about hearing that I should fast for forty days on liquids. She gave me this book that talked about the different fasts, and it had liquids only in the book. It said that a forty-day fast was to break down mental strongholds that had been built up overtime. I was in awe. This was what I needed. I had stuff that I needed to be healed from, which had developed over the years. I prepared my mind to get started right away.

I spoke to my pastor about fasting, and he told me he, too, went on a liquids-only forty-day fast. He told me it was an experience like no other. He recommended this book by Benny Hinn, *Good Morning, Holy Spirit*, as a reference along the way.

One day, in the midst of my fast, as I was lying in the bed, I heard the sound of children playing outside by my window. It was at night. I could not move, and it felt as if my body was still, but my spirit was moving out my body and heading toward the window. I just realized I was having an out-of-body experience.

I thought, *Is this what the guy in the book* Good Morning, Holy Spirit *was talking about, when you are so in tuned with the Holy Spirit that you encounter angels and can have an out-of-body experience?* As I looked out the window, I realized my body was still lying in the bed.

What I saw were white angelic figures playing outside. I felt God's presence like never before. It was strong, and I felt as if God was right there in my room. I wasn't scared or nervous; I had peace like never before. When I came to, or when the spirit came back to my body, I just laid there in total awe. I had just experienced God like never before.

When the Lord called me to fast, I hesitated at first because of the type of fast he had called me to do. I finally gave in because I would see the number 40 everywhere; it was like He did not let up, and so I had to be obedient. I can honestly say when I went through the fast, I felt like I was at my strongest spiritually. During this time, gifts where developed, bondages were broken, discernment went up, and I went to a greater level in Him. I also met my husband shortly after.

There are benefits to fasting, and we must learn to be still and hear God's voice so we can receive directions and guidance for our lives. There are many instances in the Bible where fasting and consecration unto God caused great things to come out of it; for example, Moses fasted for forty days and forty night and was used to write on the tablets the words of the covenant—the Ten Commandments (Exod. 34:28). Daniel fasted for twenty-one days and then was visited by an angel (Dan. 10:3). Queen Esther and the Jews fasted for three days before she could be used to save her people (Est. 4:15–17), and Jesus Himself fasted for forty days and forty nights before He started His ministry (Matt 4). The bottom line is that there are major shifts that take place when you deny your flesh and seek the face of God.

This was what I needed before I could fully walk in the purpose and plan God had for me. I needed to rid those strongholds that had built up over time from the negative seeds that were placed by the enemy. I am not saying that this is your course of action, but this was mine, through the leading of the Holy Spirit. Jesus said in Matthew 17:21, some things do not come out except through fasting and prayer. I needed a spiritual detox. If you are called to fast, make sure to hear from God the proper instructions, and check with your physician if you have any health problems.

By saying yes to the Lord, He has blessed me with spiritual gifts that I could not even imagine. Since then, He has also blessed me with a wonderful husband who loves and adores me and helps me raise my three children. Nine years into our marriage, I became pregnant again and birthed another beautiful baby girl. I became a minister, praise-and-worship leader, outreach coordinator, and just recently, was ordained as elder. I have a nonprofit women's group empowering women all over, I have a master's degree, I am back in school to obtain my doctorate, and now, I'm an author. In 2015, I was one of the four selected among many to be honored as an emerging leader by a prestige African American organization. I have received a proclamation from the commissioner's office and a recognition from the mayor. I have also been appointed by a president of an international honor society.

Now this is the plan that God has for me, and He is not through with me yet. I'm expecting bigger, better, and greater as I continue the path that God has set for me! My dream as a kid to save the world was not a myth; it was very true, reaching one person at a time using the gifts, talents, and positions God has entrusted me with. I came to learn the meaning of my name—I no longer hate it like I used to when I was a child. Rashieda means someone who is great, wise, and powerful. No wonder the enemy wanted to change my name to something that was less than anything great. As I look back over all I have been through in my life, I am grateful that God never left me or forsook me. Even though the enemy tried to stop me from my destiny, I was already predestined for greatness; all I had to do was to walk in it! I now understand that God allowed some things to happen in my life because it was necessary to tap into the greatness that was deep down inside me!

Obtaining Victory through Wisdom

In order for us to grow spiritually or move to another level in God, we need to obtain the wisdom of the Lord. God's wisdom is mentioned all throughout the Bible, but there is a book dedicated to the Lord's wisdom, and it's in the book of Proverbs. The word *wisdom* appears approximately 181 times in the Old Testament and 53 times in the New Testament, for a grand total of 216 times, so evidently the Lord wants us to grab understanding of this word, which aids us in living a successful life.

The word *wisdom* comes from the root word *wise*, which means to "have good sense or judgment." It also states to "be aware of what's going on, to possess inside information." If you look in the Bible at 1 Kings

3, you will find the third king of Israel, whose name was Solomon, asking the Lord to give him wisdom on how to rule over the people that he had been entrusted with. Solomon offered one thousand burnt offerings to the Lord, then the Lord appeared and asked Solomon to ask for anything he wanted, and He would grant it unto him. God is so awesome and faithful. Sometimes we need to just offer our sacrifices to the Lord—a sacrificial praise, our time, or our worship—and He would just show up and grant us our heart's desires. Solomon could have asked for anything—money, power, houses—instead, he asked for a desiring heart. He knew the tasks of being a king and a judge would require great knowledge and responsibility. He needed the Lord's wisdom to walk in the calling God had given him. That is the same way with us. We need to ask God for His wisdom to make better choices, to direct our paths, and to help us be who He has called us to be so we can walk in victory because we are walking in the divine will and purpose of God. God was so pleased by Solomon's request because he did not use his request for selfish gain, like riches or gold. God granted Solomon's request of obtaining wisdom, and He also gave him riches. God gave exceedingly abundantly to Solomon, above all he could ask or think (1 Kings 3).

Since wisdom is defined as "possessing inside information," I look at this as possessing inside information of the mysteries of God. He has made known unto us through the wisdom of His Word. We are literally without excuse on how to live a successful life because it's all laid out for us in the Bible. We just have to obtain understanding by way of the Holy Spirit.

When You Obtain Wisdom, You Get Understanding

When obtaining wisdom, one has to grasp an understanding of the Word of God. The two go hand and hand; you cannot have one without the other. I can remember when I was not walking out my salvation, which I defined as saying I'm saved but not obeying the commandments of the Lord. I was not walking out my salvation; I still did what I wanted to do. I was trying to read the Bible like a book. I would start from

Genesis and quickly lose interest when I got to the book of Leviticus. To be honest, back then, I found it to be boring. I found my lack of understanding of the Bible was due to me not asking the Lord to open the eyes of my heart to gain an understanding of His Word. It was just like I was reading words on a paper with no meaning to me at all. You know how it was in grade school—sometimes when you were asked to read a comprehensive story, you read it long enough to get the answer to the question, or you read the story and when you go back to answer the question, you can't because you forgot what you just had read. This is just how some of us read the Bible. We read it, then we forget what we have just read because we did not get an understanding. How can we prevent this from happening? In Proverbs 1:23 (NIV), it explains the solution very well. The Lords says, "Then I will pour out my thoughts to you, I will make known to you my teachings." It wasn't until I opened my heart and prayed for God to allow me to comprehend His Word that I received revelation of what I was reading. I was no longer just reading words on a paper; I was receiving instructions for my life. In order for you to walk in the victorious living that God has purposed for you, you have to obtain the wisdom of God. The Lord's wisdom will give you direction for your life. I wish I had asked for the wisdom of the Lord a long time ago; I would have not made as many mistakes in my life. If you were like me, trying to read the Bible as a book and not gaining revelation of what you are reading, ask God to open the eyes of your heart. What does this mean? This means to ask God to allow your heart to receive the scriptures and watch God make known His mysteries unto you.

As God continues to speak to you through His Holy Scripture, He will guide you on the path you need to go, and you will have victory every single time because you have God on your side!

Conclusion

This book was written on purpose for your purpose.

What was this book all about? It was about the seeds of hurt, rejection, and devaluing of your worth that have taken root in your life to stop you from walking in who you were created to be, but I came today to let you know you were created for so much more!

The enemy wants to try and kill you before you catch wind of who you are in God, but the enemy messed up because God knows you! In Jeremiah 1:5, God says, "Before I formed you in the womb, I knew you, before you were born, I set you apart; I appointed you!" This means you were predestined for greatness! *Predestine* means that you were destined for a particular purpose. Many don't reach this level because the enemy tries to come in and alter their destinies. Some things we have to go through in this life are not perfect, but take heart! We serve a perfect God! He will take all the bad you went through and turn it around for your good! Take me for example—if I had not left Chicago to go to Ohio, would I be that person living for God, let alone serving Him? If I had not gone through some of the things that I went through, would I be writing this chapter today to help someone else? I always tell people when they ask me about my past that I would not change a day in my life because I might not be the person I am today. Since we have been born, we have been faced with opposition, sets of problems, challenges, and issues we must deal with while we are living in this world. We must press on and walk in confidence that God has a set plan for our lives and push past barriers that try to block us and move forward because our destiny depends on it!

When we were children, some of us had to deal with a set of issues based on what our intellectual minds could handle at the time. Some of our problems could have been based on finding our own identity, or it could have been out of our control based on our surroundings, parents, or family issues. Most of our decisions in this stage of life were determined by someone else's decision because we were too young to comprehend our own way of life; we were being taught or shaped into what others thought we should be.

When we became teenagers, some of us had a little more autonomy because our parents or loved ones were not with us all the time. We started developing our own thought process, making our own decisions based on what we were taught as a child combined with what we learned from our peers. Our actions were shaped by what we perceive was happening in the world around us. This way of thinking has now helped shape who we thought we should be.

Then when we reached adulthood, we took what we have learned from the cradle until now. It has shaped our thought process. We think we got it all together, we think we know what we should do, and we think we are certain of the direction we should go—we know, we know, and we know!

The problem with this scenario is that along the way, just as we have learned good things, the enemy has sown bad things in our minds, which determines our actions and shaped our beliefs about who we think we are.

Let me explain. When you were a child, someone probably didn't like you for whatever reason, but in your mind, you wondered what you had done to have them dislike you, so you felt compelled to please people so you don't have to feel the negative effects of rejection. Your parents could have abandoned you or did not show you affection, or perhaps you were not picked to be in the cool kids' club, so now you have doubts about your own self-worth, leaving you to feel a sense of inadequacy. You might have been violated, which caused a sense of fear, hurt, and pain that you tried to bury deep down inside, which damaged your self-esteem and poisoned future relationships.

As a teen, you might have dealt with rejection, so you followed after the crowd even when you knew it was wrong. You made bad decisions based on others' thoughts and opinions of you. You might have stayed in a toxic relationship because of fear of being hurt, abandoned, and alone. These are the seeds that the enemy have set up in our lives to cause damage to our character and to alter our destiny

When we became adults, we do what we want to do. We got it all figured out, but little do we know, those negative seeds have set in and took root in the inner core of our souls; and it is controlling our very being. Now we have just become puppets to the negative seeds that have sprouted up, derailing our future.

The bottom line is that we all have encountered failures, disappointments, rejection, oppression, and feelings of inadequacy; and now we can't move forward because those seeds have taken root, and we are stuck not walking in the purpose that God has for us.

Well, I come today to pluck out those negative roots and tell you this very day that you were *predestined for greatness*. You must give it over to God and then walk in the plan He has set for your life! Jeremiah 29:11 (NIV) says, "For I know the plans I have for you," declares the LORD, 'plans to prosper you and not to harm you, plans to give you hope and a future.'" God has already set the plan for your life, which is greater than you could ever imagine. There is greatness locked inside you, and you must not ever forget it!

Scripture to Read before Prayer

For those God foreknew he also predestined to be conformed to the image of his Son, that he might be the firstborn among many brothers and sisters. And those he predestined, he also called; those he called, he also justified; those he justified, he also glorified. (Rom. 8:29–30 NIV)

Prayer

Heavenly Father, I pray that, on this very moment, you will show my sister or brother those negative seeds that were planted by the enemy so they can expose the plot and plan that was meant to cause their destruction. You said in Romans 8:28 that "we know that all things work together for the good of those who love the Lord and who are called according to His purpose." Let them know that they were predestine for greatness, and it was necessary for something to happen in their life for them to tap into the greatness that lies deep inside them. I cast out any demonic force or influence that tries to hold them back from the purpose and God-given plan that has been set for their life. I ask, in the name of Jesus, that You will heal my sister or brother of any hurt, pain, feelings of rejection, oppression, and abandonment that they may be facing. I speak life to every area of their life and ask that You will give them supernatural strength to deal with their current and past issues so they can move forward in You, God. I thank You, Father, in advance for the testimonies that will come from their deliverance, and consider it done in the mighty name of Jesus, I pray. Amen!

Bonus Reading

Purpose Walker

We have been on this journey called life, and I don't know about you, but ever since I was a little girl, I knew deep down in my soul that I was meant to do something great in this world. I know I am not the only one that feels this way. If you are feeling this way as well, I believe the Lord is telling you it is time to walk in your purpose! The Word of God says for every season, there is a time to do something (Eccles. 3:1–8). There is a certain season that we are supposed to be operating in what God has for us to do at a particular moment in time. God has a purpose and plan for our lives; if it wasn't so, we would not be here today. Some of us have been asking, "Lord, what do you want me to do next?" Many times, God puts purpose into our hearts. He puts that drive or passion to do something, and He puts that unction in our Spirit to do more than what we are doing at the current moment. He may show you in a dream what you are supposed to be doing for Him because He called you for a specific purpose. When I looked at this concept a little closer, I was reminded of the scripture in Genesis 1:26–28 (NLT); it says this:

> Then God said, "Let us make human beings in our image, to be like us. They will reign over the fish in the sea, the birds in the sky, the livestock, all the wild animals on the earth and the small animals that scurry in the ground."

So God created human beings in his own image. In the image of God, he created them; male and female he created them.

Then God blessed them and said, "Be fruitful and multiply. Fill the earth and govern it. Reign over the fish in the sea, the birds in the sky, and all the animals that scurry along the ground."

When you think about the word *purpose*, and when you look outside your very window, you will see purpose all around you. You will see the purpose of a tree, you will see the purpose of a house, and you will see the purpose of a car. Let's look at the purpose of a car—it is to transport you from point A to point B, and when you look at the purpose of a house, that is where you dwell in, that is where someone sleeps, and that is where they can be sheltered from the storm and the rain. Let's look at this when we think about purpose when it relates to a human being. God said in Genesis 1, "Let us make man in our own image, according to our likeness." This means we carry the very attributes of God, and one of our purposes in life is to be like our Heavenly Father. When I studied this, I looked at five attributes of God we must possess to be a purpose walker.

One of the attributes of God is diligence. When you are walking in your purpose, it is going to take some diligence; it is going to take some perseverance. What do I mean? I am saying that when you are walking in what you are called to do, it is not going to be easy. Nothing is going to happen overnight, and your purpose is not going to just fall in your lap. Diligence will be the very thing that builds your spiritual muscles. It makes you strong and ready for what you are about to encounter. When you are going through this journey called life, I have to be honest—it is not for the faint of heart. It takes strength, it takes diligence, it takes one to be focused, and it takes some planning; but the key to all of it is you have to continue to move forward. We are created in the image of God, and we are created in His likeness, which is the greatest ability that He has given us. If you remember,

He made creation in six days, and he didn't even break a sweat. If we carry the same attributes of God, He has given us the same ability to move forward with power and authority!

The second attribute is that He has given us creativity. The Bible says, "In the beginning, God created the heavens and the earth." He visualized how He wanted things to go. He visualized what He wanted the earth to look like, what He wanted us to look like, and made it happen. God has given us creativity so when we are walking in our purpose, He is going to give us the ability to go forward with diligence and to be creative about it. He will give us the tools. He will give us the plans.

Sometimes, we focus too much on what we don't have instead of what we do have. Sometimes, we just need to put one foot in front of the other and move forward in what God has for us to do, and He will do the rest. He will give us the ideas, and He will give us the fresh anointing we need to create so we can move forward in diligence. Remember, we are creative. That is the attribute He has given to us, so we need to tap into that creativity. You might be saying, "I am not creative. I am not that type of person." It's time for us to change our way of thinking. We were made in the image if God, so we are creative regardless of what we think about ourselves.

The third attribute of God is that He has a "can do it" mind-set. What does that mean? It means that our God knows without a shadow of a doubt that all things are possible through Him. If we carry the same attributes as God, we also should adopt a "can do it" attitude. God has given you the ability to do that very thing He has called you to do. I am reminded in Numbers 13:30, the Israelites were promised a land flowing with milk and honey, but their enemies were occupying the land. They wanted to go into the land flowing with milk and honey, but the people were murmuring, saying, "We can't do it. We can't beat those giants." Then one stood up and said, "We are able to do it!" This is what God has instilled in us. He has given us the "can do it" mind-set, so when we are faced with a hard thing, when we are faced with that thing that seems impossible, we move forward not based on our own capabilities but because we serve a possible God. He has a "can do it" attitude, He never uses excuses, and He always finishes what He started; and we must possess that same mind-set.

When you are walking in your purpose, the enemy is going to try and stop you from advancing forward. This is his job. His job is to kill, steal, and destroy (John 10:10). If that is his job, he is going to do everything he can to steal your purpose, kill your dreams, and destroy your destiny at all costs.

So if we know that the enemy is on his job, we have to be on our job. We must proclaim that the enemy is under our feet, that God has given us the ability to trample over serpents and snakes (Roman 16:20; Luke 10:19). We have to have the mind-set that we cannot be defeated.

I made my mind up a while back that I am going to change my way of thinking concerning the situations that happened in my life. Instead of saying, "Wow, the enemy is just having his way," I am going to say, "You know what? God must be working at something great in my life right now, and it is going to be a blessing that is going to come out of this situation." When you are going forth in your purpose, the truth is you are going to have some challenges. You are going to have things that try come in your way to try and block you from your purpose, but God has given you the ability to conquer those things. You need to have a "can do it" mind-set and believe that all things are possible through God who gives you strength.

The fourth attribute of God is that we serve an honest God. We need to be honest with ourselves. We must be honest with everything that we do. We serve a God that cannot lie; His Word is the truth. So we need to be honest with ourselves. What is that thing that is holding us back from walking in our purpose? We need to be honest about the issues that we are dealing with because God knows our issues anyway. He is a God that knows all and sees all. If He is a God that knows all and sees all, why are we being dishonest to ourselves?

Once we are honest with ourselves, God is able to come in and help us overcome that very thing that is holding us back from our purpose. In these particular times, we have no time to waste, we have no time to lose, and we need to go forward in what God has called us to do.

We need to acknowledge and rid those things that are holding us back from walking in our purpose. We need to be honest with ourselves just like God is honest.

The fifth attribute of God is His generosity. He created the world for us. As God was generous to create the whole world for us, we should be generous with our gifts and talents.

My grandmother always told me that if I focused on doing God's work, then God will deal with my stuff. When we focus on our purpose, and we are being generous to others, giving out of our hearts, God will deal with our stuff. When we are consumed with our own issues and circumstances, we delay being used to help someone else because all our time is focused on our own issues.

So what does the Bible say about our purpose? Genesis 1:28 (NIV) says, "Then God blessed them and said, 'Be fruitful and increase in number.'" This means that whatever you set out to do, if it is in God's will, He will bless it. You will be fruitful in that very thing He has given to you. Even when you go to Genesis 9:28, when the world was destroyed by a flood and it was just Noah and his family, God gave the same decree. He said, "Be fruitful and multiply, subdue the earth, overcome it, I gave you dominion." So whatever you are purposed to do, you will be fruitful in it, and if it is not flourishing, you need to check the tree. Maybe something is wrong deep down in the root that needs to be dug up. In Mark 11, Jesus saw a fig tree that wasn't bearing any fruit, and He cursed it at the root, saying, "You will bear no more." When something is not bearing fruit, you need to check it.

I am always checking myself; I am always checking the fruit in me. I pray to the Lord, saying, "If there something in me that needs to be removed and I don't know about it, God, I need for you to take it out."

Sometimes, we need to be honest with ourselves as one of our attributes is honesty. We need to be honest with ourselves and get rid of those things we know means us no good. Oftentimes, we want God to do the miraculous in our lives, but are we willing to do what it takes to receive it? We must stay in right standing with God. How can God fully operate in us if we are not abiding by His Word? We must make sure we are bearing good fruit. We have to ask ourselves, "What is the fruit that people are seeing within me? Am I a reflection of Jesus Christ? Or am I reflecting the opposite of Him."

God is an awesome god, and He has given us the ability to go forward in what He has called us to do—not our will, but His will. When our will lines up with God's will, it is when we will produce much fruit. So I challenge you to walk in your calling that God has for you because everyone on this earth has a purpose.

In this season, God is raising a might army for Himself, and we need to make sure we are in right standing with Him. We need to make sure His Word is evident in our lives and we bear fruit of His word. We need to make sure we are bearing good fruit.

I challenge you to take time and meditate on what some things in your life are that need to be cut off. Are you bearing good fruit? Are you operating in the attributes of God so you can walk in the purpose that God has for you?

Seed Sowing

Have you ever wondered if all the good things you have done in life will pay off one day? Have you ever invested in something and did not get a return on what you have invested? Well, I'm here to let you know that when you invest in God, you will always reap a harvest!

Sometimes we get weary when we have made steps toward success and have not seen the fruits of our labor yet. I say *yet* because many times we work hard, set goals, help others, and follow the Word of God, but we still do not see the break we have been looking for. Even though many of us have experienced this, it is important to stay the course because it doesn't mean that our breakthrough is not on the way.

One day, when I was in prayer, I heard the Lord say this to me: "Continue to plant and take care of what was planted. For your harvest will soon come." As the Lord spoke this to me, I believe the same for you! When you think about one who plants, you have to consider all the effort that goes into planting something. You need to consider the seed that you are planting, if it has special instruction to help it grow. Is it in the right soil? Does it have the right temperature? Is the dose of sunlight right for this particular seed? Does it need a large amount of water? Does it need a minimal amount of water? The bottom line is that the seed is not going to grow overnight; it's going to take some time, and it's going to take some effort to care of what was planted.

When you take care of what was planted, that seed will start to grow, but when it grows, you have to continue to take care of the seed until it makes its full transformation into its purpose. I am going to read to you Galatians 6:9 from the NLT version: "So let's not get tired of doing what is good. At just the right time we will reap a harvest of blessing if we don't give up."

The King James Version says, "Let us not be weary in doing well for in due season, we shall reap if we faint not."

What is the Lord trying to tell us? He is saying, "You have been planting the seed. You have been taking care of what was planted. You will reap a harvest if you don't give up." We cannot give up on those seeds God has put in our lives, those seeds He has given us to manifest at a later date. You cannot give up in this season; you have to continue to take care of the seed. You have to continue to plant, you have to continue to water, and you have to continue to take care of what God has given you because, just like the Word said, you will reap a harvest if you faint not. It's always a stipulation when it comes to His word, so what are you going to do? Are you going to faint? If so, you will not see the harvest. Then the Word of God tells us, "Do not be weary in well doing." This means that whatever God has given you to do, don't get tired and don't get frustrated because those frustrations will cause you to faint. God is also telling us that He has given us the strength to go through what we need to do, so don't stop sowing seeds of faith, joy, happiness, graciousness, and love because those seeds will manifest into something great if you faint not.

When you are trying to walk in your purpose, when you are trying to rediscover your passion, guess what? It's going to take some time. When you look at the farmer as he plants seeds, those seeds are not going to grow overnight, but the farmer is going to continue to take care of what was planted and wait in expectation for a harvest. If you do not continue to water or nurture a seed, it will not grow. God has given us seeds in our lives to grow and manifest into something great. You might be someone who has had your seeds in the soil for a long time, but be encouraged; your harvest will come because the Word of God says so, and we hold on to that promise. Also, you need to be careful when you are planting that seed; you have to make sure you have it in good soil. That means it does not matter how good the seed is if you do not have it in the right soil. It will not grow, so watch who, where, and what you invest in—people, places, and things—and make sure you are led by God. Also, you should be careful who you share your seeds with because that seed is not meant to be shared with everybody. What does that mean? It means some people are going to carry or support your vision, but some may want to see your vision fail. But guess what? We serve a God that knows all and sees all, so we pray to God for protection, we pray to God for guidance, and we pray to God to protect the seed, protect the gift that is in our lives.

Protect your seed; check the soil. Is the soil good? Because if the soil is not good where you are planting, you better remove it and plant it somewhere else because the enemy comes to steal, kill, and destroy; and the enemy wants to destroy those seeds that God has given you. When a farmer plants, they have to make sure the ground is tilled first. When someone is tilling the ground, it is dirty, it is messy, and it takes a lot of hard work. But guess what? It is getting ready for that seed to be planted and to bloom into a harvest that will shock the world. In this season, regardless of what we see around us, when we look at situations and it seems like things are not moving, trust in God's Word that, in due season, we will reap a harvest.

I have been planting a seed over my kids for a long time. I pray this prayer over them because I know if I pray this one prayer, everything else will line up. I say, "Lord, let them come to have a personal relationship with you because if they have a personal relationship with you, they will know you, and they will have everlasting life." So I continue to water the seed of salvation in their lives until I see the manifestation come to pass.

In due season, you are going to reap a harvest, and you are going to see the fruit of your labor. If you continue to complain, murmur, and doubt God, then you are going to delay your harvest. Things will try to come to knock you on your back, but guess what? We serve a God who says, "I have made you more than a conqueror." We have to believe what His Word says. If I am more than a conqueror, then that means I can conquer any situation that comes my way. I am going to continue to plant the seeds, I am going to continue to take care of the seeds, and I am going to continue to wait for the seeds to manifest in my life, in my family's lives, in my city, and in this country until I see a transformation. I am not going to be worried about what is going on because I serve a God that sits high and looks low. It might sound cliché, but that is so true. God is high above the heavens, and He is looking down at us. He has made us a little lower than angels and crowned us with glory! He has given us dominion; He has given us power, and He has given us authority to trample over scorpions and snakes so we walk in reassurance that we will see the promises of His Word come into our lives.

We don't always know what avenue God is going to come into our lives, but we stand on the promises of God. When we stand on the promises of God, it reduces our anxiety and frustration. We might not understand all that God is doing in our lives, but we hold on to the fact that all things work together for the good of those who love the Lord and is called according to His purpose (Rom. 8:28). Everything God does is good because He knows what is best for us when we don't even know ourselves. We often say, "Lord, direct my steps," but when He takes us in the direction we should go, we then ask God, "Why am I here?" He then has to remind us, "You told me to direct your steps. So I am going to direct you the best way I know for your life and for your benefit." This means that just because it's not the path of least resistance, it does not mean it's not the path that God has given us to take.

Listen, the Lord is telling us today, "Do not be weary in this process. There is no time to get weary. You are going to reap a harvest." It might be tomorrow—what if you give up today and your harvest is the very next day, just around the corner. You will miss it because you fainted. God is telling us He has given us specific instructions in His Word for us to follow. He says, "Do not be weary, for in due season, those seeds that have been planted in our lives, those seeds that I have given you, will manifest. They will." He didn't say maybe; he didn't say sometimes. He said, "You will reap a harvest if you faint not." So hold on until your promise comes.

Walking in True Compassion

What do you think the word compassion means? Having compassion means putting yourself in someone else's shoes; showing empathy, love, respect, kindness; being patient with yourself and with others; and not being judgmental. When you look at Jesus's life, He showed compassion toward all who struggle with issues. He extends this same compassion to us even today, so who are we not to show compassion to others?

There are two stories in the Bible that I want us to focus on. One is called the prodigals son and the second one is called the adulterous woman. The prodigal son is found in Luke 15:11–24 (NLT), and it says this:

To illustrate the point further, Jesus told them this story: A man had two sons; the younger son told his father "I want a share in your estate now before you die" so his father agreed to divide his wealth between the sons. A few days later, the son packed all his belongings and moved to a distant land and there he wasted all his money on wild living. About the time his money ran out, a great famine swept the land and he began to starve. He persuaded a local farmer to hire him and the man sent him into the field to feed the pigs. The young man became so hungry that even the pods he was feeding the pigs looked good to him, but no one gave him anything. Finally, he came to his senses he said to himself, at home even the hired servant has enough food to spare and here I am dying of hunger. I will go home to my father and say, "Father I have sinned against you both heaven and you and I'm no longer worthy of being called your son please take me on as a hired servant." So he returned home to his father and why he was still a long way off his father saw him coming, filled with love and compassion he ran to his son, embraced him and kissed him. His son said to his father, "I have sinned against both heaven and you and I am no longer worthy of being called your son." But his father said to the servant, "Quick, bring the finest robe in the house and put it on him, get a ring for his fourth finger and sandals for his feet. Kill the cow we have been fatting we must celebrate a feast. For this son of mine was dead and now he has returned to life, he was lost but now he is found." So the party began.

We are going to look at this from two angles. When you look at the prodigal son, he knew he had an inheritance. The father was preparing something for him. When you look at the prodigal son, he wanted to do things his way; he wanted to rush the process. Sometimes when we are trying walk in our purpose and trying to rediscover our passion, we try to reach our destiny really quick, but we must be careful when we're moving forward in our purpose, in our passion to reach our destiny, that we don't do it without God.

Sometimes we get ourselves in situations where we get a big head and kind of lose our way. Sometimes we might have things happen to us to cause us to think the things we have done in our past have been so bad that we missed God and we cannot go back to the place that He restored us before. The prodigal son had experienced this phenomenon. He went out, he wanted his inheritance, he wanted it now, he rushed the process, he failed, and he lost his way. If we are honest, some of us have experienced this very scenario. The prodigal son spent all his money on wild living. He reached rock bottom, and when he reached rock bottom, he was so sorrowful of himself that the pig slop looked good to him. Sometimes I can concur that in my life, I have been in situations or circumstances where I have hit the bottom and I am sorrowful, asking God, "How did I get here?" But the Bible said the prodigal son came to his senses, and that was the blessing he needed to bring about repentance and change. We must not live in regret from the things that has happened in our lives because, just like the prodigal son, it can cause us to come to our senses and bring about repentance and change. I feel sorry for the ones who don't come to their senses; they continue to follow the road of no return and head for destruction.

Another thing about the prodigal son we need to pay attention to is that he didn't feel worthy to come back home to his father. He spoke this to his father, "Disown me as your son. I know I have done this terrible thing. I have sinned against you, I have sinned against *God*. Hire me on as your servant. I will be a servant. I don't want anything else." This is what the enemy wants us to feel when we get off the path that God has for us; he wants us to feel ashamed and condemned. We have to understand that God is a forgiving god, and regardless of the things we have done that we're not proud of, we have a loving Father with arms open wide, ready to embrace us.

I love the Lord, and I thank Him for His compassion and His love toward us. We, too, need to have compassion on ourselves. We cannot live in regret for the things that we have done in our lives. Just as God has forgiven us, we have to forgive ourselves because God loves us so much He does not want us to stay in regret. He doesn't want us to remain in shame and doubt because if we do, we will not be able to move forward in the plan that God has for our lives.

This story also shows us that we need to have compassion for others. The prodigal son's father did not remind him of his wrongdoing and said, "You shouldn't have done this. Oh, look at you, you've reached rock bottom now, and you want to come back?" He didn't say any of that. He saw his son from a far-off distance and said, "This is my son—he is coming home."

This is how God treats us. Even when we feel we are far off from God, God looks at us and says, "There's my son, there's my daughter," and welcomes us with open arms. There is a celebration that is going to take place—another son or daughter is returning back to the Lord!

The story also shows us that we must have compassion on others. Every one of us will go through our own faults, failures, issues, and circumstances, so who are we to judge and not have love and forgiveness toward someone else's issues? The prodigal son was welcomed by his father with open arms, so if you look at people who have hurt you, who have wronged you, and who have done you wrong, will you walk in the same love and forgiveness? We ourselves have done things that we are not proud of, so who are we to sit up there and judge and mock others and make them feel worse than what they already feel? We need to embrace them, we need to love them, we need to consider that they have gone through the faults and failures of life, and most of all, we must forgive them and welcome them with open arms. That's what our heavenly Father does toward us, so we need to show that same type of love and compassion. There is such a lack of compassion and love in this world that is unbelievable. Regardless if we don't agree with another person's views, it doesn't mean we should judge and not show love and compassion toward them. Christ showed love and compassion; it was one of the things he showed us throughout the Bible—that we need to love those who have wrong us.

There is a scripture in the Bible that talks about "love those who have hurt you, bless those and pray for those that persecute you" (Luke 6:28). It's important because we cannot live with a bitter or unforgiving heart. When you let bitterness and anger dwell in your heart, you cannot move forward in the things of God, and you cannot walk in the purpose of God.

The second story that shows the act of being compassionate is the story of the adulterous women found in John 8:1–11 (NLT) and it says this:

> Jesus returned to the Mount of Olives but early the next morning he was back again at the temple, a crowd soon gathered, and he sat down and taught them. As he was speaking, the teachers of the religious law and the Pharisees brought a woman who had been caught in the act of adultery and they put her in front of the crowd. "Teacher," they said to Jesus, "this woman was caught in the act of adultery, the law of Moses says to stone her. What do you say?" They were trying to trap him into saying what they will use against him but Jesus stooped down and wrote in the dust with his finger. They kept demanding an answer, so he stood up and said, "All right, but let the one who has never sinned throw the first stone," then he stooped down again and wrote in the dust. When the accusers heard this, they slipped away one by one beginning with the oldest until only Jesus was left in the middle of the crowd with the woman. So Jesus stood up said to the woman, "Where are your accusers? Didn't even one of them condemn you?" "No Lord," she said, and Jesus said, "Neither do I. Go and sin no more."

If we are going to be Christlike, if we are going to walk in His characteristics, we need to have compassion toward others. This adulterous woman committed adultery, so here the Pharisees and the Sadducees and the religious officers followed the Law of Moses. So it says in the Law of Moses, "a woman who commits this act, let them stone her." So here was Jesus in the midst of the crowd, in the midst of all these people, and they wanted to stone her. They said, "Jesus, what would you do? Do you dispute the Law of Moses?" Jesus did not answer their questions, but they kept on pressing Him, so He replied, "If you are without sin, then you throw the first stone."

Who are we to judge? We all have sinned and come short of the glory of God. There's no sin that is greater than the next, so who are we to condemn and judge someone? This is not having the attribute of Christ. If Christ showed compassion, then who are we not to show compassion?

This reminds me of the scripture that says, "Same way you judge others you'll be judged in the same manner." This scripture is found in Matthew 7:2. He gave us these examples in the Bible so we can apply it to our lives. When you look at the life of Jesus Christ he was often sitting in the midst of sinners, and the saints—the Pharisees, Sadducees, and religious officers of the law—were questioning him saying, "Why are you sitting with those sinners? Why are you over there? You should be with us." He replied, "I did not come for the well, I came for the sick" (Mark 2:17). We're supposed to show compassion to others regardless of their issues and their circumstances. So if we're going to be a reflection of Jesus Christ, if we are going to operate in our fullness of Him, we have to have the compassion of Christ. If He judged us on everything we have done, guess what? We would be goners, but His Word says, "He throws our sins as far as the east and the west." This means it is gone, and we must have compassion toward ourselves for the things we are not proud of, and we must have compassion on others. We do this by forgiving ourselves of our mistakes and failures moving forward and by having compassion on others—not being judgmental, not holding forgiveness or grudges in our heart, but devoting ourselves to prayer and loving others despite their faults and failures while allowing God to work in the areas that need fixing in their life.

In these times, we have to combat all this hate with love, respect, and kindness. We must not condemn ourselves or condemn others but show compassion as the Word commanded us to. If we're going to walk in the attribute of Jesus Christ, then we must show love and compassion in a world where there's so much hatred. We must be the light that Jesus talks about—the light in the midst of darkness—and take a stand so others will follow.

Scriptures for Meditation

Meditation on the Mind

Do not conform to the pattern of this world but be transformed by the renewing of your mind. Then you will be able to test and approve what God's will is—his good, pleasing and perfect will. (Rom. 12:2 NIV)

You were taught, with regard to your former way of life, to put off your old self, which is being corrupted by its deceitful desires; to be made new in the attitude of your minds; and to put on the new self, created to be like God in true righteousness and holiness. Therefore, each of you must put off falsehood and speak truthfully to your neighbor, for we are all members of one body. "In your anger do not sin "Do not let the sun go down while you are still angry, and do not give the devil a foothold. Anyone who has been stealing must steal no longer, but must work, doing something useful with their own hands, that they may have something to share with those in need. Do not let any unwholesome talk come out of your mouths, but only what is helpful for building others up according to their needs, that it may benefit those who listen. And do not grieve the Holy Spirit of God, with whom you were sealed for the day of redemption. Get rid of all bitterness, rage and anger, brawling and slander, along with every form of malice. Be kind and compassionate to one another, forgiving each other, just as in Christ God forgave you. (Eph. 4:22–32 NIV)

We demolish arguments and every pretension that sets itself up against the knowledge of God, and we take captive every thought to make it obedient to Christ. (2 Cor. 10:5 NIV)

Set your minds on things above, not on earthly things. For you died, and your life is now hidden with Christ in God. When Christ, who is your life, appears, then you also will appear with him in glory. Put to death, therefore, whatever belongs to your earthly nature: sexual immorality, impurity, lust, evil desires and greed, which is idolatry. (Col. 3:2–5 NIV)

Finally, brothers and sisters, whatever is true, whatever is noble, whatever is right, whatever is pure, whatever is lovely, whatever is admirable— if anything is excellent or praiseworthy—think about such things. (Phil. 4:8 NIV)

Therefore, prepare your minds for action, keep sober in spirit, fix your hope completely on the grace to be brought to you at the revelation of Jesus Christ. (1 Pet. 1:13 NIV)

For those who are according to the flesh set their minds on the things of the flesh, but those who are according to the Spirit, the things of the Spirit. For the mind set on the flesh is death, but the mind set on the Spirit is life and peace, because the mind set on the flesh is hostile toward God; for it does not subject itself to the law of God, for it is not even able to do so, and those who are in the flesh cannot please God. (Rom. 8:5–8 NIV)

Meditation on Strongholds

For though we live in the world, we do not wage war as the world does. The weapons we fight with are not the weapons of the world. On the contrary, they have divine power to demolish strongholds. We demolish arguments and every pretension that sets itself up against the knowledge of God, and we take captive every thought to make it obedient to Christ. (2 Cor. 10:3–5 NIV)

No weapon forged against you will prevail, and you will refute every tongue that accuses you. (Isa. 54:17 NIV)

Put on the full armor of God, so that you can take your stand against the devil's schemes. For our struggle is not against flesh and blood, but against the rulers, against the authorities, against the powers of this dark world and against the spiritual forces of evil in the heavenly realms. Therefore, put on the full armor of God, so that when the day of evil comes, you may be able to stand your ground, and after you have done everything, to stand. Stand firm then, with the belt of truth buckled around your waist, with the breastplate of righteousness in place, and with your feet fitted with the readiness that comes from the gospel of peace. In addition to all this, take up the shield of faith, with which you can extinguish all the flaming arrows of the evil one. Take the helmet of salvation and the sword of the Spirit, which is the word of God. (Eph. 6:11–17 NIV)

He replied; I saw Satan fall like lightning from heaven. I have given you authority to trample on snakes and scorpions and to overcome all the power of the enemy; nothing will harm you. (Luke 10:18–19 NIV)

"Truly I tell you, whatever you bind on earth will be e bound in heaven, and whatever you loose on earth will be f loosed in heaven. "Again, truly I tell you that if two of you on earth agree about anything they ask for, it will be done for them by my Father in heaven." (Matt. 18:18–19 NIV)

No temptation has overtaken you except what is common to mankind. And God is faithful; he will not let you be tempted beyond what you can bear. But when you are tempted, he will also provide a way out so that you can endure it. (1 Cor. 10:13 NIV)

They triumphed over him by the blood of the Lamb and by the word of their testimony. (Rev. 12:11 NIV)

I have told you these things, so that in me you may have peace. In this world you will have trouble. But take heart! I have overcome the world. (John 16:33 NIV)

The thief comes only to steal and kill and destroy; I have come that they may have life and have it to the full. (John 10:10 NIV)

Meditation on Fear

The Lord himself goes before you and will be with you; he will never leave you nor forsake you. Do not be afraid; do not be discouraged. (Deut. 31:8 NIV)

Say to those with fearful hearts, "Be strong, do not fear; your God will come, he will come with vengeance; with divine retribution he will come to save you." (Isa. 35:4 NIV)

But now, this is what the Lord says— he who created you, Jacob, he who formed you, Israel: "Do not fear, for I have redeemed you; I have summoned you by name; you are mine. When you pass through the waters, I will be with you; and when you pass through the rivers, they will not sweep over you. When you walk through the fire, you will not be burned; the flames will not set you ablaze. For I am the Lord your God, the Holy One of Israel, your Savior. (Isa. 43:1–3 NIV)

I sought the LORD, and he answered me; he delivered me from all my fears. (Ps. 34:4 NIV)

Even though I walk through the darkest valley, I will fear no evil, for you are with me; your rod and your staff, they comfort me. (Ps. 23:4 NIV)

For the Spirit God gave us does not make us timid, but gives us power, love and self-discipline. (2 Tim. 1:7 NIV)

David also said to Solomon his son, "Be strong and courageous, and do the work. Do not be afraid or discouraged, for the LORD God, my God, is with you. He will not fail you or forsake you until all the work for the service of the temple of the LORD is finished. (1 Chron. 28:20 NIV)

When I am afraid, I put my trust in you. In God, whose word I praise— in God I trust and am not afraid. What can mere mortals do to me? (Ps. 56:3–4 NIV)

Do not be afraid of those who kill the body but cannot kill the soul. Rather, be afraid of the One who can destroy both soul and body in hell. (Matt. 10:28 NIV)

So do not fear, for I am with you; do not be dismayed, for I am your God. I will strengthen you and help you; I will uphold you with my righteous right hand. (Isa. 41:10 NIV)

Meditation on Purpose

For in him all things were created: things in heaven and on earth, visible and invisible, whether thrones or powers or rulers or authorities; all things have been created through him and for him. (Col. 1:16 NIV)

"For I know the plans I have for you," declares the LORD, "plans to prosper you and not to harm you, plans to give you hope and a future." (Jer. 29:11 NIV)

But you are a chosen people, a royal priesthood, a holy nation, God's special possession, that you may declare the praises of him who called you out of darkness into his wonderful light. (1 Pet 2:9 NIV)

Great are your purposes and mighty are your deeds. Your eyes are open to the ways of all mankind; you reward each person according to their conduct and as their deeds deserve. (Jer. 32:19 NIV)

And we know that in all things God works for the good of those who love him, who have been called according to his purpose. (Rom. 8:28 NIV)

I know that You can do all things, and that no purpose of Yours can be thwarted. (Job 42:2 NIV)

"Before I formed you in the womb, I knew you, before you were born, I set you apart; I appointed you as a prophet to the nations." (Jer. 1:5 NIV)

Meditation on Forgiveness

In him we have redemption through his blood, the forgiveness of sins, in accordance with the riches of God's grace. (Eph. 1:7 NIV)

Get rid of all bitterness, rage and anger, brawling and slander, along with every form of malice. Be kind and compassionate to one another, forgiving each other, just as in Christ God forgave you. (Eph. 4:31–32 NIV)

For if you forgive other people when they sin against you, your heavenly Father will also forgive you. But if you do not forgive others their sins, your Father will not forgive your sins. (Matt. 6:14–15 NIV)

Therefore, if anyone is in Christ, the new creation has come: The old has gone, the new is here! (2 Cor. 5:17 NIV)

As far as the east is from the west, so far has he removed our transgressions from us. (Ps. 103:12 NIV)

So watch yourselves. "If your brother or sister sins against you, rebuke them; and if they repent, forgive them. Even if they sin against you seven times in a day and seven times come back to you saying, 'I repent,' you must forgive them." (Luke 17:3–4 NIV)

Meditation on Love

Love is patient, love is kind. It does not envy, it does not boast, it is not proud. It does not dishonor others, it is not self-seeking, it is not easily angered, it keeps no record of wrongs. Love does not delight in evil but rejoices with the truth. It always protects, always trusts, always hopes, always perseveres. Love never fails. But where there are prophecies, they will cease; where there are tongues, they will be stilled; where there is knowledge, it will pass away. (1 Cor. 13:4–8 NIV)

For God so loved the world that he gave his one and only Son, that whoever believes in him shall not perish but have eternal life. (John 3:16 NIV)

Dear friends, let us love one another, for love comes from God. Everyone who loves has been born of God and knows God. Whoever does not love does not know God, because God is love. This is how God showed his love among us: He sent his one and only Son into the world that we might live through him. (1 John 4:7–9 NIV)

"You have heard that it was said, 'Love your neighbor and hate your enemy.' But I tell you, love your enemies and pray for those who persecute you, that you may be children of your Father in heaven. He causes his sun to rise on the evil and the good and sends rain on the righteous and the unrighteous. If you love those who love you, what reward will you get? Are not even the tax collectors doing that? And if you greet only your own people, what are you doing more than others? Do not even pagans do that? Be perfect, therefore, as your heavenly Father is perfect. (Matt. 5:43–48 NIV)

But God demonstrates his own love for us in this: While we were still sinners, Christ died for us. (Rom. 5:8 NIV)

Above all, love each other deeply, because love covers over a multitude of sins. (1 Pet. 4:8 NIV)

"Teacher, which is the greatest commandment in the Law?" Jesus replied: "'Love the Lord your God with all your heart and with all your soul and with all your mind.' This is the first and greatest commandment. And the second is like it: 'Love your neighbor as yourself.' All the Law and the Prophets hang on these two commandments.'" (Matt. 22:36–40 NIV)

Husbands love your wives, just as Christ loved the church and gave himself up for her. (Eph. 5:25 NIV)

Dear children, let us not love with words or speech but with actions and in truth. (1 John 3:18 NIV)

Prayer of Salvation

This prayer is intended for those who do not know the Lord and want to have a personal relationship with Him. This prayer is also for those who once knew Him but went off the path and want to come back to Christ. This is for those who would like to rededicate their life to Jesus Christ and make Him their Lord and Savior. This is also for those who have been caught up in religion but do not have a personal relationship with God. If you fit in one of these categories, then pray this prayer with me:

> Dear Heavenly Father, I know I have sinned against you. I repent for my ways—please forgive me. I believe that You sent Your only begotten son, Jesus Christ, to die for my sins. He rose again in three days with all power and took the keys from death, hell, and grace for my sake.

> Lord Jesus, please come into my heart. Make me whole. Set me on the straight and narrow path that You have placed for me. Give me a deep hunger for Your Word. Give me wisdom and understanding of Your Word. Show me my purpose. Send godly people in my life that I can grow with. I have faith that I will be what You called me to be and do what You called me to do.

I thank You in advance for my next level in You. I pray all these things in the name of Your Son, Jesus Christ. Amen.

If you prayed this prayer, you are saved! Join a Bible-believing church and get active! Walk in your purpose! If you prayed this prayer, please contact us at contact@rashiedatimpson.org. We want to pray with you and give you some additional information on living a saved life.

Love you in Jesus's name!
Rashieda

Chapter Notes for Study

Chapter One: There Is Greatness Locked Inside You

Chapter Two: The Early Years

Chapter Three: A Dark Moment, Then a Glimpse of Light

Chapter Four: Seeds of Rejection

Chapter Five: The Move

Chapter Six: Losing Who I Was Created to Be

Chapter Seven: False Love

Chapter Eight: The Transformation

_____

_____

_____

_____

_____

_____

_____

_____

_____

_____

_____

_____

_____

_____

_____

_____

_____

_____

_____

_____

_____

_____

_____

_____

Chapter Nine: The Victory

References

King James Bible
New International Bible
New Living Translation Bible
Christian Standard Bible
English Standard Version
https://environment.org/2019
https://www.biblestudytools.com/
https://biblehub.com/
https://www.christianity.com/

Biography

Rashieda F. Timpson was born in Chicago, Illinois, and spent her childhood there until unforeseen circumstances forced her to move to Toledo, Ohio. During her teenage years, she continued to face many obstacles and struggled to find her identity, which led to substance abuse, bad relationships, and poor decisions.

She always had a connection with God, praying at a young age, but did not develop a relationship with God until her mid-twenties, when she had an encounter with the Holy Spirit that changed her life forever. Because of the struggles and issues she has faced, she feels compelled to be a spokeswoman for Jesus Christ and has been called to devote her life to the mission of service.

She is a goal-driven woman who is passionate about helping others reach their full potential, with hopes that they would one day become successful.

She also has a strong desire for people to live a healthy lifestyle (mind, body, and spirit), which compelled her to earn her master of science in nursing degree with a specialization as a family nurse practitioner.

Rashieda has also earned a business design and life coach certification to assist with the vision to help individuals from all different walks of life and backgrounds. She is the founder and CEO of a nonprofit organization called United Sisters (Women Inspiring Women), which is an assembly of women coming together to encourage, uplift, inspire, and service others with love and integrity.

Her vision behind this organization is for women to strive to be better mothers, daughters, wives, friends, and leaders as God directed their path and gave them the knowledge and the initiative to do so. Rashieda encourages women to rise up and know their worth—that they are precious in God's sight—and be confident that they are beautiful, successful, intelligent, creative, anointed, and innovated. This organization has outreach programs, empowerment calls, and conferences to help all; it's not just limited to women.

Rashieda was licensed as a minister and ordained as an elder under the leadership of Willie C. H. Garrett, pastor. Rashieda has been commissioned to preach the gospel and encourages people to strive toward new heights even through adversity like the scripture says in Philippians 4:13 (NIV), "I can do all this through Him who gives me strength." She is the spokesperson for Rashieda Timpson Ministries, preaching and teaching the Word of God with clarity, insight, and understanding.

Rashieda is a phenomenal speaker, life coach, preacher, teacher, and writer who is passionate about Jesus and helping His people tap into the greatness that is inside them while helping individuals strive toward a deeper relationship with the Heavenly Father.

Rashieda Timpson Ministries Contact Information

To contact Rashieda Timpson Ministries for prayer requests, testimonies, upcoming events, book releases, or booking for your next event or conference, please go to www.rashiedatimpson.org or email us at contact@rashiedatimpson.org. We look forward to hearing from you!

CPSIA information can be obtained
at www.ICGtesting.com
Printed in the USA
BVHW030955180719
553829BV00003B/69/P

9 781796 044225